MY
FATHER
WHO IS
NOT IN
HEAVEN

If there are no dogs in Heaven,
then I want to go where they went.
　　　　　　　　　—Will Rogers

Have fun—if not, you'll bore us.
　　　　　　　　　—Hermann Hesse

Nothing is ever so sad you can't find something
funny in it, and nothing is ever so funny
you can't find something sad.
　　　　　　　　　—Henry Sinton

MY
FATHER
WHO IS
NOT IN
HEAVEN

Patricia Adler

Patricia Adler

Writers' Block
Berkeley, California

Publication data
Adler, Patricia Sinton, 1941–
   My father who is not in heaven / Patricia Adler
   p. cm.
   ISBN: 978-0-9634167-9-7 (pbk. : alk. paper)
   1. Adult children of aging parents—Family relationships. 2. Jewish Wit and Humor. I. Title.

Cover canine silhouette by Sergey Lavrentev
Interior canine silhouette by Jan Camp

Cover and book design by Jan Camp
www.arclightbooks.com

Printed in the United States of America

Published by

Writers' Block
2904 Avalon Avenue
Berkeley, California 94705

writersblock71@gmail.com

www.myfatherwhoisnot.com

For Matias, Eleanor, Zachary,
and their cousins

The Sinton family, 1947

Contents

Glossary of Yiddish Terms

schmendrick   a pip-squeak; a no-account; a kind of shlemiel—but weak and thin

schmutz   dirt, filth

shabbes   sabbath

shiksa   a non-Jewish woman, especially a young one

shlemiel   a foolish person; a consistently unlucky or unfortunate person; a clumsy, gauche type; anyone who makes a foolish bargain

shvartzer   a derogatory term for a black man

utz   to goad, to nag, to needle

verklempt   choked with emotion

Preface

Dad becomes the mensch I want him to be when he tells a Jewish joke. That is why, during his last tumultuous years, I videotaped him in "performance." I was hoping to transport him to happier times. He always said, "No matter how bad you feel, Jewish humor makes your spirits rise."

My project did not go as I expected. Though I set out to be Dad's stenographer, I became more fascinated by real life unfolding. I began to chronicle his off-camera behavior, especially his dramas and tirades. It soon became clear that a conventional family portrait could not capture the volatile essence of Henry Sinton. To know him was to hear him, so I offer here an enhanced soundtrack of life with Dad.

Because truth really is stranger than fiction, I have not changed any names except two. I have dragged this project out over so many years that most of the central players are now dead. I have written the stories that reach far back in time in the past tense, but I keep the drama of our last two decades in the present tense to give a sense of time as it was unfolding. The uncertainty and urgency of cascading events collapsed the distinctions between past, present, and future. Forces seemingly beyond our control trapped us in the precipitous present.

Faithful to my intention, I let Dad's jokes steal the spotlight between my chapters. They stand alone even without his personal embellishments, and you may prefer to read only them.

This is my send-off for Dad, my perverse Muse, who often berated us, "Listen to me! Listen to me!"

Yes, Dad, we're still listening.

Pat Adler
Berkeley, California
2012

Star of the Show

July 1993

"Shut up!" Dad yells from the TV room as the barking dogs and I barge up the stairs. "Can't you see I'm watching?"

He sits on the edge of his chair, an elbow on each knee, leaning so far forward that his face almost grazes the TV screen. He holds the VCR remote in his left hand and raises his right with index finger poised. He is watching his favorite performer: himself.

Mom joins me in the doorway. "See? He's transfixed. He does this every day."

"Every day?"

We snort in disbelief. I had no idea when I set out last summer to videotape Dad telling his jokes that he would be the prime viewer, his own best audience. After we had filled four videotapes, I made dubs for him to keep. Here he sits watching a scene filmed in 1992 beside his and Mom's swimming pool at their country house in Sonoma. The same dogs, his Sweetie, my Lizzie, lie at his feet. On film Dad stares straight into the camera, his bright blue eyes bulging with anticipation. My camera zooms in jerkily. His face fills the screen, fuller than it is today, his blond good looks lasting well into old age.

Dad, the viewer, nods back at himself, beaming expectantly, like a paid prompter ready to jump in should the star falter. But this star never does. His timing is exquisite, his Yiddish accent convincing, and the delivery of the punch line a bull's-eye.

Dad leaps to his feet, silently mouthing the finale: *Sure Heifetz is a good fiddler, but I like Shapiro better. When Shapiro plays, I sleep with his wife!*

"Perfect!" Dad shouts. "Damn that was good. Don't you love it?"

Dad waves his arms above his head and dances in a circle. The dogs explode in a frenzy of celebration, cigarette ash raining down upon them.

"Goddamn I'm good. I'm great."

Watching his self-applause, I realize that I have inadvertently killed the video project. In a high-tech version of Narcissus, Dad has become so enamored replaying himself on videotape that he's stopped compiling stories for a new one. I will have to settle for reruns.

The Condo on Riverside Drive

This is a story about Abe and Sadie Schwartz, who live in a condo on Riverside Drive. Abe and Sadie have been married forty-eight years, a devoted couple. Abe made a good living in the rag trade. Raised two beautiful kids. Always observed Shabbes, very good Jews.

They live in a big building overlooking the Hudson River. Used to be very fancy, 100 percent goy, until the Crash of 1929. Gradually, Jews started moving in. First one, then two, and now it is 99 percent Jewish, all except for one Mr. Smith on the tenth floor.

One day at breakfast Sadie says, "I wonder why that nice Mr. Smith is still living here after all the other Gentiles have moved out?"

"I don't know," says Abe. "I'll try to find out."

Next evening Abe and Mr. Smith ride up in the elevator together.

Abe says, "Mr. Smith, you have lived in this building longer than anyone else. All the other goys left a long time ago. Pardon me for asking, but we always wonder, why do you stay?"

"Well, Mr. Schwartz, I'll tell you. When I moved here in '28, I swore I wouldn't leave until I've had intercourse with every lady in the building. I'm proud to say I have only one more to go."

"Oh, I see. That's very nice," says Abe as he gets off at his floor and hurries home to the apartment to tell Sadie.

3

"Sadie, guess what? I just rode up in the elevator with that fancy Mr. Smith, and he tells me why he's still here. He says he's not moving until he's shtupped every lady in the building, and—can you believe?—he has only one more to go!"

"Aha!" says Sadie. "It must be that stuck-up Mrs. Epstein on the sixth floor!"

Baalshamin, the Golden Dove

In my recurring dream Dad is a golden dove teetering on a perch in a gilded cage. I see with some alarm that his feathers are fading from bright, golden yellow to white.

"My name is Baalshamin," trills the dove, bobbing its head and sidestepping toward me. He lowers his head and presses against the bars of the cage. "Tickle my neck. There, harder! Scratch my back. Lower! Now rub my head. Yes!"

I am charmed. I have never met such an articulate bird. The more I do Baalshamin's bidding, the brighter his color grows. He keeps repeating his name and tells me how to assemble all the doodads in his cage. The mirrors need polishing. Bells and rattles have to be rehung where he can reach them. He wants the paper on the floor to be changed and the stand-up toy soldiers rearranged in marching formation.

I am amazed by his fastidiousness and want to work quickly to please him. I take on tasks Baalshamin hasn't requested. The food dishes need washing, so I clean and refill them. Then I notice that the drink dispenser is empty.

I ask Baalshamin if water goes in the bottle, and he says, "No. Nectar."

I am delighted with his intelligent wit and affectionate nature and don't want any harm to come to him. If I take good care of him, he will stay sweet and strong. The more I do, the more he sings . . .

Dad's hair is white now. He hasn't stopped drinking, even though Mom's been trying to "fix him" for sixty-three years. One of his last friends died yesterday. I know he is sad, so I visit. He is in the living room, small and stooped in his enormous armchair. The TV news is blaring. He cannot see or hear me coming. I approach his chair, careful not to bump his glass of vodka, "hidden" within reach behind the upholstered skirt.

I lean over to kiss his cheek. My hair brushes his hearing aid, and it starts to shriek—short, piercing bursts of alarm.

"I'm sorry, Dad."

"What? I can't hear a fuckin' thing."

I hug him, and through his tweed coat my hands feel the bones of his back. The sharp ridges of his scapulas flutter just like bird wings.

Not Very Nice

1949

Once upon a time, cocktails brought my family to life. My grandmothers drank martinis before lunch, scotch on the rocks before dinner. Ritualized drinking defined adulthood, and those who couldn't keep up, like Mom, had to be careful not to be a spoilsport. Alcohol gave her headaches, so she'd nurse her glass of wine while smoking and playfully dishing out the juicy gossip and barbed banter.

During long cocktail hours at our grandparents' gatherings, I and my ten-year-old cousins, John and Tom, roughhoused behind the sofas and reread the tattered pile of comic books: *Nancy and Sluggo*, *Little Lulu*, *Donald Duck*, and my idol, *Red Ryder*. With all my heart I longed to be his sidekick, Little Beaver. The bond between Red Ryder and Little Beaver eclipsed all others. With each rereading I became Little Beaver, loyal and brave. At home I wore an Indian headdress of dyed eagle feathers and a holster with a loaded cap gun. In my reenactments Red Ryder provided adventure and protection, both. I imagined that he loved me. "You betchum, Red Ryder!"

Our parents' animated babble and laughter played like a well-worn record in the background. Formal dinners were regular events on both sides of my large, ingrown German Jewish family. Mom's mother, Gaggy, had us over for dinner every other Sunday night, and she always hosted a Christmas night banquet with a final round of presents for everyone under a sparkling Christmas tree. Dad's parents, Nana and Poppa, had us over for sit-down dinners every other month as well as for a matchless Thanksgiving feast cooked by Henri Tarnac, a professional chef, and served by his wife, Louise, and her sister, Angele. I can't remember ever celebrating the Jewish holidays.

At our gatherings everyone spoke at once, brandishing wit and judgment without restraint. The grown-ups lived for entertainment and lavished it on one another, especially on birthdays, anniversaries, and homecomings from trips. These were the days before television, and my relatives, whom Dad called "the jumping up and down crowd," filled the vacuum with celebrations of themselves. They elevated teasing to performance art, composing skits with more than a dozen cast members. Their performances captured each other's foibles, mimicking their patter and trivial preoccupations. They roared at their own cleverness.

An old script typed by Auntie Nell on yellowing onionskin paper portrays me at the age of nine. The occasion marked my parents' return from a trip to Mexico in 1950. The scene is Dad's office at the Walter family firm, where both he and brother Stanley worked:

Pat: I don't see why Daddy complained so much about his work and made me come down here every day while he was away. I'm missing three weeks of school, and if I don't get straight As this month he won't have anything to talk about ever. (telephone rings) Yes, Dad. . . . No, Dad. . . . Yes,

Dad. . . . No, Dad. . . . Yes, Dad. . . . No, Dad. . . . Yes, Dad.

Faith (his assistant): Pat, I don't see how you do it. You've finished a whole week of Henry's work in one hour.

Pat: Faith, you haven't mentioned Daddy's name for the last fifteen minutes.

Faith: Henry Sinton, Henry Sinton, Henry Sinton, Henry Sinton.

Pat: That's better.

The grown-ups monopolized center stage all their lives. It was a birthright. They never questioned their entitlement, nor did we. We children existed to amplify them, to grow up to be like them. They needed us to reflect back the best qualities in themselves.

Sometimes in the midst of conviviality came a furious outburst, usually from Dad or an aunt or uncle. Their tempers were sudden and savage and struck with no warning. We would look up from our comic books, holding our breaths, electrified by the charge in the room.

"Shut up, Henry. You don't know what you're talking about."

"I don't need advice from any of you."

"Stop it."

"Shhh."

"You shush, you sonsofbitches!"

The fights were usually verbal and short-lived. The most memorable ones ended with a slap or with a drink being thrown in someone's face. But then the party would continue. No one ever left. It made no sense to us on the other side of the sofa. An explosiveness lurked beneath the gaiety, and a quickness to ridicule made it unsafe to ask an innocent question. We were supposed to be born know-it-alls.

My relatives' inexplicable eruptions are probably what prompted my brother, Peter, and me to make up rescue and survival games. In the privacy of our bedrooms we played Newborn Half-Dead Baby. Being three years older, I got to play Mother, with Peter perpetually cast as a baby who had just fallen over Niagara Falls. I would pull him from the churning water, bandage all his wounds, and nurse him back to health.

"Ag'in, Paddy, do it ag'in," he would say afterward, and we did.

We made up endless rounds of Good Mother/Bad Mother. Peter, who also obligingly played a starving orphan, went from door to door begging the resident mothers for food and shelter. I enacted different kinds of mothers, progressing from the bad, cruel mother to an indifferent but dutiful one and, finally, to the ideal nurturer—generous, loving, playful, and completely available. At this point in the game, Peter, undone by my excessive kindness, would burst into tears crying, "No, no, Paddy, that one is *too nice*."

How could anyone be *too nice*? In our family *nice* was highest praise. I worked hard to act *nice*, especially when the volatile adults around us did not. I deeply believed that if I behaved well, they would too, as if our fragile ship would fly apart if I erred. *Be nice*, above all, *be nice*.

There was a heavy price to be paid for not being nice. In 1944, when I was three, we were renting Auntie Marge's house near Carmel Beach while Dad attended naval officers' training in Monterey. One morning some neighbor girls and I were digging a network of tunnels at the beach when I suddenly needed to run home to go to the bathroom. I began to pack up my pail and shovels and strainers, but Mom would not hear of me taking them.

"No, you're coming right back."

"I don't want them to touch my things."

"It's not nice to be selfish! You must share."

When my protest turned to tantrum, she gave away all my sand toys on the spot.

What lesson did I learn? Get duplicates! By the time I started school two years later, I brought two boxes of crayons: an old, jumbled one with blunted points to share and a new box with sharp points perfectly aligned just for me. I became known as a *nice* girl.

But how nice is *nice*? I knew I was not as nice as I pretended to be, but was that nice enough? Did I have to be nice all the time without any reservations? The more I puzzled over it, the more *nice* transcended etiquette. It verged on the heroic. It required an element of human sacrifice, an annihilation of will and personal desire. *Nice* never says no. *Nice* is quick to smile. *Nice* is selfless. *Nice* responds instantly to every command, just as Little Beaver would. *Nice* trained my inner lifeguard to live on high alert: to listen and watch before speaking, to drop everything and rush in whenever calamity called. *Nice* will make the world safe. *Nice* will disarm the critics and the furies. *Nice* will buy love.

But *nice* could not change Dad. *Nice* could not distract him long enough to listen. *Nice* could not convince him that it's poisonous to play favorites. All those years at the family dinner table, we sat there like Stooges: Dad at the head, his beady hawk eyes on Peter to his left. Mom, on his right, and I, to her right, were safely out of range.

I think it was Peter's open-mouth chewing when he was six or seven that most provoked Dad, or maybe the humming pleasure Peter took in eating and touching the food with his fingers. Dad would suddenly slam his fist onto the table or slap Peter and bellow, "You goddamn pig, look at the mess you're making. That's no way to eat!"

And we all just sat there stunned. Peter never cried. I froze in my chair. Mom never said anything nor changed the seating arrangement, but she bought yards and yards of plastic sheeting to protect Peter's chair from spills.

Two Bad Parrots

Poor Mrs. Goldfarb is tearing her hair out over her two female parrots. Such a problem! Whenever she invites company to her house, they whistle and shriek, "Hey, we're hookers. Wanna have some fun?"

No matter what Mrs. Goldfarb does, she cannot break them of this bad habit. Finally, she consults her rabbi.

He listens patiently to her story, then says, "I have two male parrots, very good African grays. They study Torah and speak Hebrew and English fluently. Why don't you bring your two parrots to my house to meet them? Maybe mine will teach yours some good habits."

Mrs. Goldfarb is delighted, and on the appointed day she arrives, schlepping her parrots in their big covered cage. The rabbi shows her to his living room to meet his two parrots. Each one wears a yarmulke and a tallis and holds a prayer book in one foot. They share the same perch as they daven over their books praying aloud.

Mrs. Goldfarb takes the cover off her parrots' cage, and her bad girls whistle and shriek, "Hey, we're hookers! Wanna have some fun?"

One of the rabbi's good parrots looks up, turns to his brother, and says, "Itzhik, get rid of the fuckin' book. Our prayers have been answered!"

Cook a Turkey, Be a Man

November 1996

The more deaf and blind Dad gets, the more ferociously he cooks. He cooks only meat, and he likes to do it alone. In his culinary ardor Dad becomes what he cooks: on his eightieth birthday I watched him scuttle around the kitchen like a lobster, boiled red, eyes bulging. On the Fourth of July he splashed about the barbecue, as silver and battle-scarred as the king salmon he was basting, swatting me out of his way with long-handled tongs. But today is Thanksgiving morning, and he is definitely a bird, beady eyed and beak nosed, his head bobbing with every movement, his scalp pink as a buzzard's beneath his transparent white hair. He has consented to show me how he prepares the turkey, so long as I remain seated on a kitchen stool out of his way.

"Women don't understand meat," he bellows. "Not lamb, not beef, not chicken, and especially not turkey. Never have. You can't trust a woman to do it right."

He's been up most of the night, bathing the turkey in a tub of warm water.

"She buys frozen turkey," he mutters. "The fool, the goddamn fool."

He soars out of reach, high on his own bombast. I cannot find the piercing words to blast him out of the sky and bring him back to earth like the wild ducks he brought home from Poppa's club when I was small. They tumbled, warm, damp, and limp, from the burlap sack onto the garage floor. I arranged them by sex: the splendid males in one row, their drab mates in another. The drying blood smelled sweet, turned sticky black.

Dad plucked and gutted the birds himself. He chopped off the mallards' emerald heads and the sprigs' gray feet. He proclaimed these ducks—mallards and sprigs—to be the best eating, then widgeon, then teal. He was a terrible shot, he said, hated that part of it, and left the killing to others. He made a point of keeping the gun at the club.

"Too bad you weren't born a boy," he'd often say. "Terrible to be a girl."

"Why?" I asked once.

"Because women have to be passive. It's a waste. You should have been a boy, and Peter with his shyness should have been a girl."

So we were both defective.

Now at the kitchen counter Dad dries the inside of the turkey carcass with a special chamois: "Not paper towels—they leave lint."

"Sniff it," he says, dandling the naked turkey in front of my face. Its bony bottom smells of herbs.

"Mmmm, poultry seasoning?" I ask.

"God, no! Nothing prepared. I pick and pulverize sage, rosemary, marjoram, chervil, and summer savory fresh from the garden."

He puts the turkey back in its roasting pan and wipes his hands on his stained khakis. He massages more olive oil into the puckered folds of turkey skin. "These poor legs," he says, fondling a drumstick in each hand. "They get so dry. Look, I made them leggings." He holds up a pair of cut-off cotton socks. "You don't want the dark meat to cook too fast."

"Nice."

"Better than nice. Brilliant. I'm goddamn brilliant."

Dad struts to the stove to taste the giblet gravy.

"The best! I'm the best!" he clucks. He spoons the stuffing into the cavity, puffing himself up as he recites the ingredients: chestnuts, celery, onion, Italian sausage, sage, parsley, cornbread.

"Don't rush a bird or question a man," he says. "Never ask where he's been. Men don't like it, and you don't want to know."

From my stool in the middle of the kitchen, I pretend to be an anthropologist, silently observing the last remnant of a doomed, chauvinistic culture. What kind of a Neanderthal is this? Just as I am thinking, *When he dies, I won't miss a thing except the chestnut stuffing,* he lifts the turkey, tin cradle and all, and waltzes in dainty circles around me. He closes his eyes and whistles through his teeth a reedy rendition of Souza's "Stars and Stripes Forever."

The first time he ever sang it to me, I was playing in the bathtub, age three. He danced a mock soft-shoe on the white-tile floor and sang:

> Be kind to your fine-feathered friends.
> That goose might be somebody's mother
> Who lives in a place called a swamp
> Where the weather is cold and damp.

He wanted me to admire his new navy whites before he shipped out to Okinawa. As an officer on a supply ship, he got to keep house for the men who had to fight and die.

Dad could crow like a rooster, cluck like a hen, and sing every word of Danny Kaye's "Minnie the Moocher," "The Fairy Pipers," and "Anatole of Paris." When he was away, I replayed Danny Kaye's brittle 78s on my record player until the phonograph needle wore down to a stub. Danny's coy grin on the album cover merged with my memory of Dad. I saw the same mischievous eyes, the same wavy blond hair, the big nose, and the exaggerated expressions.

After the War Dad taught me to swim the Truckee River rapids. He'd been a college swimmer and could slice through any water with ease. I would hold onto his back as he swam the breaststroke upstream along the back current in our icy, teal-blue swimming hole. At the top, where the river narrowed and white rapids churned, Dad would plunge from a rock into the waves. I felt completely safe as we bounced and swirled downstream to the shallows.

These days Dad cooks for the dying. In a doomed two-year effort to get his brother Bobby to gain weight, Dad keeps preparing codfish balls, a childhood favorite. After one especially triumphant lunch, he phones to crow that Bobby ate a pound and a half of codfish balls. "Imagine that," he repeats, "a pound and a half of food at one sitting!"

Now Dad's whistling "Rock-a-Bye Baby." I am not sure when the melody changed, but it occurs to me during this pause in his bluster that I still long to love him. Perhaps with a different soundtrack, we could have conversed. Dad always says, "Do as I say, not as I do." But at this moment in his kitchen kingdom, stripped of the plumage of youth, the pomp of war, and the blare of his bluster, it's the reverse: do as he does, not as he says.

He tucks the turkey back into its pan. He straightens the socks around the drumsticks and pats a blanket of buttered cheesecloth gently over the breast. His fragile sweetness silences me as much as his loud harangues ever did, and I don't make a peep.

# Long Island Duck

Bella Mendelbaum lives on the Lower East Side. Every Friday afternoon she goes to her friend Buxbaum the butcher to buy a Long Island duck to cook for special Shabbes dinner. She can count on Buxbaum. His Long Island ducks are the best.

But on this particular Friday, Buxbaum isn't there. A new butcher is filling in.

"Shalom, young man. I'm Mrs. Mendelbaum. My friend Mr. Buxbaum always saves a Long Island duck for me."

The young butcher goes to the refrigerator room in back and brings out a nice fat duck and sets it on the counter.

Mrs. Mendelbaum spreads its legs, sticks her nose in the cavity, and sniffs.

"No, I'm sorry. This is not a Long Island duck. It's from New Jersey."

The butcher returns it to the refrigerator and comes back with another, which he presents for her inspection.

Mrs. Mendelbaum leans over and takes a whiff and says, "Sorry, Sonny, this duck is from Pennsylvania. Definitely not Long Island."

Once again he returns the duck and brings out another.

Mrs. Mendelbaum repeats the procedure and sniffs.

"Yes! This is a Long Island duck. This one I'll take."

While the butcher is wrapping it for her, Mrs. Mendelbaum asks, "You're new around here?"

"Yes," says the young man.

"So where are you from?"

The butcher turns around, bends over, spreads his buttocks, and says, "You tell me, lady!"

Duck, Duck, Goose

1960

At the airport as I was boarding the plane for college, Dad said, "Don't turn into a Radcliffe man."

With no time to ask what he meant, I marched to my window seat, half expecting to sprout chest hair and a beard. Dad's warning stayed with me for years. My tongue could not form words to argue—with him or any other man. By the time I'd begun to find my own voice, Dad was growing deaf and couldn't have heard me if he'd wanted to.

I have been reluctant to admit the power of Dad's words. I wanted them to roll right over me—quick harmless nothings. After all, don't words vanish into thin air the instant they're uttered, especially if we refuse to respond? Isn't it a sign of weakness to allow ourselves to be hurt? I felt deep shame when, as a very small child, I'd burst into tears of rage when Mom or Dad ridiculed something I said or did. When I told them that they had hurt my feelings, their response was always the same: explosive laughter.

"We've hurt her feelings! Can you imagine? Hurt her feelings." And their laughter would reignite until Mom could catch her breath to say, "No, don't feel that way!" It was confusing to be told by higher authorities how I should and shouldn't feel. Obviously I wasn't doing it right, so I worked hard not to react.

"The only trouble with you," Dad would tell me when I was in high school, "is that you are sometimes haughty."

I know he is remembering the time when I was fourteen and defied him. I had been upstairs in my room happily doing homework when he called from the living room to come down immediately to watch a ballet that was on television. I resented the interruption but came downstairs with my book. The furniture was arranged in such a way that I could settle on the floor in front of the television and behind a loveseat that shielded me from Dad's view. I continued reading. Dad got up from his armchair to see what I was doing and exploded.

"Get out of here! Go upstairs."

"That's exactly what I want to do," I said as I walked out of the living room.

Dad tore after me and kicked me in the fanny.

"You make me so goddamned mad!" he shouted. I kept marching, haughty dignity intact, as if neither his words nor his foot had made an impact.

Privately, I scrutinized that cocktail hour outburst: the first time Dad had ever directed his bullying rage at me, his favorite. Dad represented all men to me back then. This incident showed me that I could infuriate him. My words had power. I concluded that men were vulnerable, easily threatened, and vicious when thwarted. They needed women to comfort and agree with them. Argument would render me permanently undesirable. To be loved would require capitulation.

My experience at Radcliffe reinforced this pathetic notion. Orientation Week was completely disorienting. Radcliffe freshmen were required to pose stark naked for posture pictures. At the appointed hour we took off our clothes in the gym's locker room and wrapped ourselves in robes or towels. Then we lined up around the perimeter of the basketball court, three hundred of the nation's supposedly brightest women, passively watching as one by one each classmate took her position behind a screen in the middle of the gym. She disrobed and faced two P.E. instructors who took notes at a table while a standing, hooded photographer snapped two pictures, one full frontal, the other profile. No one refused. I stifled my objections and mirrored my classmates' compliance. I felt stripped of much more than clothes. The practice continued until 1962. I later learned that Harvard men routinely raided the vault in the Radcliffe athletic department to steal the pictures.

In Cabot Hall, my dorm far from home and far from Harvard Yard, women brandished their sharp wit in private. Among ourselves it was hip to be outspoken, liberal, irreverent, and Freudian. But in class with Harvard men, most of us acquiesced to our more voluble male classmates. The more I parroted my patriarchal instructors (never a woman or a rebel among them), the better my grades got and the more invisible I felt.

I typed long, ponderous papers, peppered with footnotes. My titles reveal how slavishly faithful I stayed to my sources: "Freedom and Authority in Political Institutions Based on the Ideas of Alfred North Whitehead" or "A Marxist's Critique of De Tocqueville's *Democracy in America*." My own words were never enough. I compiled massive bibliographies for added clout, but to me my overblown treatises resembled failed male impersonations.

Mom and Dad sent letters that said, "To thine own self be true." I had no idea what they were talking about. What self? That had gone the way of lost luggage. I didn't want a self; I wanted a boyfriend.

Three months into my freshman year, my periods mysteriously stopped. By the time the school year was over, I had gained twelve pounds. (I weighed more than I eventually did when I was full-term pregnant.) While my sexually active dorm mates were terrified of becoming pregnant, I secretly feared that I never would.

The summer after freshman year I lived at home and worked as a receptionist in a windowless office for a Liebes department store executive. It was the dreariest time of my life. I bought a long-sleeved, brown knit dress from Women's Apparel on the second floor with my first paycheck and wore it every day to work. I was the reincarnation of Auntie Mame's drab Agnes Gooch. When I told Mom and Dad about my amenorrhea, they were very worried and sped me to an endocrinologist.

The doctor prescribed an endocrine test that required me to collect every drop of urine over a twenty-four-hour period in a large jar. It was then to be fed or injected into some poor sheep for divination. My endocrinologist's office was downtown in the 450 Sutter skyscraper where Dad had business. He offered to deliver it for me on his way to work. It was early when Dad left off the jar of urine. The office was not yet open, so Dad placed it in the hall beside the locked door. Unfortunately, he was on the wrong floor, and the endocrinologist never received my specimen.

In the course of our inconclusive, summer-long search for my missing periods, I never put together the obvious: Dad's haunting warning at the airport the day I left for college, "Don't turn into a Radcliffe man," had become for me a posthypnotic suggestion.

Thanks Heaven

Sam Ginzberg works in the rag trade downtown on Seventh Avenue. He's been married to Bekeleh for thirty-five years. He works hard, makes a good living, but lately he's been dying for this gorgeous blond shiksa who runs a shop across the street. He's been trying to get in her pants, and finally after six months he does.

A week later he's pissing fire and goes to his doctor.

The doctor says, "Sam, you got a dose of the clap. What're you going to tell Bekeleh?"

Sam thinks, then says, "Well, I've been pretty faithful to Bekeleh 'til now. We have a good marriage. I'll go home and tell her."

Sam gets back to their apartment on Riverside Drive.

"Bekeleh, have I got a surprise for you!"

"Oh, Sam. How wonderful. What is it?"

"A case gonorrhea."

"Oh, thanks God, I'm so tired from Manischewitz."

Dead Baby

2000

This morning Mom phones to report a senior moment from the night before after she'd driven home from a restaurant.

"Your father had a complete fit because he thought I'd parked too close to his car in the garage. He was screaming so loud that neither of us realized I hadn't turned off the engine. It idled all night with my key in the ignition. Alex (their cook and driver) discovered it when he came to cook breakfast. It took all day to air out the house!"

Later Peter phones from work to report that Dad's been eighty-sixed from Liverpool Lil's, the same saloon where Dad lost both his car and his false teeth last year. Peter had had to drive him around the next day in search.

"I'd better go check on them."

You would never know from outward appearances that we are falling from grace. Mom and Dad still live at 2 Laurel Street in the handsome, three-story, redwood house that they remodeled in the late 1940s. Its huge plate-glass windows overlook the San Francisco Presidio, the bay, and the Golden Gate Bridge to the north. The interior spaces are open and free, with few walls and no hallways. It is sunny and brilliant by day, theatrical by night. Inset halogens spotlight their contemporary crafts and paintings. Walls the color of artichoke and upholstery fabrics of gray-greens, rose, ochre, and sienna complement the dazzling kilim rugs and form a perfect backdrop for the highly polished English and American antique furniture. Along the east wall of the living room are floor-to-ceiling shelves of hardback books and pale birch cabinets that house a wet bar and a large television.

Mom and Dad's shared love of textiles and fine design deepened over the course of their long marriage. Mom became an accomplished weaver and fiber artist, and Dad worked for thirty years in her family's wholesale carpet and upholstery business, D. N. & E. Walter.

Dad is deeply sloshed by the time I arrive in late afternoon. A blue haze of cigarette smoke hangs over his armchair like a malevolent halo. He is, in a perverse way, protected. Pickled and smoked, he has triumphed over the rest of us. Mom's brief fling with Al-Anon in the early '90s fizzled out. Neither Peter's log of Dad's whereabouts and alibis nor my letters beseeching Dad to stop drinking ever produced a desired effect. What point is there now in telling an eighty-year-old that his drinking and smoking are killing him? In truth, they're killing us. Mom's weariness seldom lifts, Peter has never been heavier, and I perform like a jittery high-wire acrobat.

I fan a clearing in the smoke and lean over to kiss Dad hello.

"Wait, wait! Hearing aid adjustment," he says pushing me away.

Sweetie is flying from sofa to chairs in ear-splitting glee. She nips at my hands and feet, then snuffles in my bag for something to eat. Finding nothing, she keeps barking. Dad kicks at her with one of his enormous shoes but misses.

"Goddamnit, Sweetie, shut up!" he screams. "An hour ago I told her you were coming, and she hasn't let up."

"Why tell her? It's not fair to rev her up, then kick her."

"I don't need criticism from you. I get enough of that from Her."

I am supposed to be his constant ally. He interprets my silence as agreement, but it is merely energy conservation. Sweetie and I settle on the sofa and soothe each other.

Mom soaks in the bath upstairs, preparing herself for another volatile dinner. She insists on eating with Dad at the big dining room table. It would look bad if the help saw them eating separately.

Dad swallows the last of his vodka on the rocks and lights another cigarette. "Listen to me," he begins. His mostly blind eyes shift focus as if seeing into the past. He's been thinking about the baby who died, a premature girl born after me. It was wartime, and they were stationed in Monterey. Mom went into labor two and a half months early and delivered a healthy three-pound baby girl. The doctors said she wouldn't live long enough to be transferred to a better-equipped hospital up in San Francisco, but as it turned out, she lasted two or three days on her own.

"Poor little thing," says Dad. "I hate to think of her alone and nameless all these years, lying there in a Monterey cemetery so far away. These days she would have lived."

"Well, Dad, what are you going to do? Name her? Wasn't she going to be Katherine or Sarah?"

"I wanted Sarah. Your mother wanted Lily."

He rises unsteadily from his armchair to make himself another drink, and I am thinking, *Yes! Another child is what they need, especially a doting daughter.* I imagine my sister as she would be today: a compliant woman of fifty-seven, single and living at home with them—the sweet daughter who would coddle them like babies.

"She must have been strong to have lived two days," I say. "Was she in an incubator?"

"How should I know?"

"Didn't you see her?"

"No, what was the point? It was hopeless."

"You never saw her? Did Mom?"

"No, of course not. The doctors said it was hopeless."

"Did anyone feed or hold her?"

"Now stop it. How should I know?"

"She probably starved—"

"Shut up and listen to me. I have a plan. . . . Alex can drive me to Monterey. With a shovel and a plastic garbage bag, we'll find the plot and dig her up. I want to bring her to the family vault in San Bruno."

"But, Dad, that's grave robbing! You can't do that. Besides you'll never find it."

"That's what you think. For God's sake, I'm no fool. Here, read me this." He ruffles through his jacket pockets and produces a folded, yellowing notarized deed stipulating the exact plot in a cemetery in Monterey.

"Dad, you're supposed to be blind."

"I know, but I can find things. Now read it to me, goddamnit."

"It says on November 12, 1943, you paid six dollars for a burial plot in the Cemeterio El Encinal . . . lot 8B, block 59. . . . Would you like me to phone the county and get permission to transfer the remains?"

Dad has risen from his chair and is pacing back and forth embellishing his reverie:

"I will dig her up, poor little thing. She'll be in a little box, probably no bigger than a shoebox. Alex will carry it back to the car. Then we'll drive to the Home of Peace, and we'll put her in there next to Michael and Stanley and Poppa and Uncle Binkus and Nana. We'll have everybody all together . . ."

Dad's trembling fingers press together as he talks. They look so soft and helpless, like little chipmunk hands. Dad's voice purrs kindly as he warms to his patriarchal fantasy.

"We'll give her a name, anything your mother wants, and have it inscribed on the marble plaque in front . . ."

Dad's eyes are misting up, and I imagine he is looking into the cold, dark vacant vault that awaits him, as lonely and alone as Mom was in her labor room while he went out drinking with Stanley. It was customary in our family for brothers to go to bars together while their wives were in labor. How hard it was for them to account to their own father, who had fathered four sons, when their wives produced daughters.

"I can't believe you woke me in the middle of the night just to tell me you had another girl," said Poppa upon being told of the birth of his second granddaughter.

A memory that I want to bury resurfaces. When Dad finally got back to the hospital after my birth, he was so startled by the first hideous sight of me that he said, "Well, she can always learn to walk backwards." Walk backwards! It is a story he often tells because he is so pleased with his numbing quip. Why have I never told him how much I hate it? Why am I sitting here listening to a maudlin drunk? Because, I assure myself, words don't leave a mark.

Dad is saying, "It's a shame, such a shame. These days she would have lived . . ."

And I imagine how *he* could have lived and what I long to tell him:

You could have lived more consciously. You could have been different from your father, just as Peter and I have chosen to be different from you.

You wake each morning, bright eyed and pink, with a whole day ahead as fresh and full of possibility as a newborn baby's. You whistle brightly as you dress and sing endearments to Sweetie. You are blessed with energy and a brain that works. Each day you can choose how to live.

You preach to us about filial love, how we should honor and love and forgive you because you stayed the course. You didn't squander the family money. You provided for our material security and planned wisely for the financial future, and for all that we thank you truly.

You demand undivided attention, which we give anxiously. How is your mood this day? Is it safe to drop our defenses, or is one of us in your crosshairs? Now, watching Dad light another cigarette, I wonder how can I lessen his discomfort. Will it make him happy to tell a story?

"Hey, Dad, remember that one about Naughty Pierre?"

"Ah, yes. But of course! Zis one is your favorite."

He rises from his armchair and morphs into a beseeching Frenchman. I see the ingratiating raconteur of old. The space between us becomes a stage, and I try again to be lulled by Dad's performance. Sing, Baalshamin, sing!

Naughty Pierre

The English teacher at L'École des Enfants en Paris has given her pupils an assignment: use the word p-r-o-b-a-b-l-y in a sentence. She calls on Naughty Pierre.

"Oui, Madame?"

"Please stand up and read your sentence to the class with the word p-r-o-b-a-b-l-y."

Naughty Pierre gets up from his desk, clears his throat, and speaks:

"Yesterday I am going down ze stairs to, to ze music room and ze door is closed but it is ze matin, I mean ze morning, and ze door should be open so I am looking through ze keyhole and I am seeing Mademoiselle Fifi is raising up her skirts and she is taking down her panties and Director Monsieur du Pont he is taking off his belt and dropping his trousers and I am thinking pro-bab-ly zey are going to shit in ze piano.

Marvelous Marius

Marius of Marseille is boasting zat he has ze biggest penis in all of Europe.

"When eet is erect, fourteen blackbirds can stand on eet wis wing feathers barely touching!"

"Mon Dieu, zat is not possible!" says Naughty Pierre.

"Well, ze last one has to stand on one leg, eet is true."

Hide and Seek

"What makes a person get like this?" Mom asks, as if she is an innocent bystander. The question is a tired quiz, usually uttered midway through a difficult dinner within earshot of Dad. It fades away unanswered when he is present, but if he has already stormed away from the table, the rest of us take stabs at answering.

"Ever since he started drinking," says Peter. "How long ago was that?"

"Everyone drank. Henry couldn't hold liquor as well as others did. It got worse when he left D. N. & E. and went into commercial real estate. Sometime in the late '50s," says Mom.

"But, Mom, he was unhappy long before that," says Peter. "Was he ever happy at D. N. & E.?"

D. N. & E. Walter had been founded in San Francisco in 1858. As with most family businesses, the pioneering fervor of its founders had dissipated by the third generation. To make matters worse, the Walters had produced daughters but no sons to take over the business. It was unthinkable in our family for women to understand and have a voice in money matters. Daughters were meant to be artistic housewives who married businessmen. Whenever conversation turned to finance and business, Mom scurried from the room. If I hung around to listen, I felt comfortably invisible.

Dad would pat my hand and say, "Don't worry about money. You'll never have to put your hand to your pocket."

This didn't strike me as condescending. I felt relieved that I didn't have to go into the harsh world to compete. I could parlay my love of school into teaching someday, and I would develop my skill at cartoon caricature to keep family members well amused. Their explosive laughter was as intoxicating to me as it was to Dad. We grew up on it, a substitute for mother's milk, and we forever foraged for more.

The directors of D. N. & E. Walter had to resort to sons-in-law to keep the business a family affair. In 1930, John I. Walter, the president of the company, was dying of kidney disease. Dad's oldest brother, Stanley, became engaged to Mom's oldest sister, Nell. After his father-in-law died, Stanley went to work for the company. At the age of twenty-one he became vice president, and by the end of World War II, he catapulted to president and kept that sinecure for the next forty years.

Under Stanley's and cousin Stephen Walter's long tenure, D. N. & E. changed from a producer of durable goods to a holding company. It held all of us in check. John I. Walter's widow, who was my grandmother Gaggy, and her generation depended on dividend income from the company to maintain their comfortable lifestyle. But these elders would inevitably start dying. Stanley and Stephen's main mission seemed to be to avoid declaring the value of the shares as a way of reducing impending estate taxes. Quarterly dividends to family shareholders bought our silence, and for decades we deferred.

"We'll always have a job for you," Stanley and Stephen assured Dad, but that job led nowhere. For three years before he went to war, Dad put tickets on swatches of material.

"Dad never liked working at D. N. & E.," Peter persists.

"That's not true," says Mom. "He loved textile design. He founded the Walter 400 line, remember?"

Walter 400 was high style and innovative with stylish showrooms at Jackson Square in the city and on Rodeo Drive in Beverly Hills. Stanley and Stephen pressed Dad to travel to promote it. Mom bitterly resisted. I overheard their tearful row in the kitchen when I was ten. Mom won, and Dad capitulated.

"Stanley and Stephen were sons of bitches," she says. "Henry would have had to travel half the year. When he refused, they brought in Herb Stein to run the fabric department, and Henry was humiliated."

I refrain from pointing out Mom's part in this, partly to keep the peace but mostly because it is hard to recall Mom in her prime, at her fiercest. Her sense of humor had been bitingly quick and to the point. Dad labeled her the funniest person in the family, "certainly the most original." And the most curious, I would add. No one could ferret out personal information from people as effectively as Mom. My school friends enjoyed her intimate interrogations and opened up to her eagerly. With her prying questions Mom got others to do the talking but seldom revealed much about her private self. My own son, Peter, later regretted that he never had a chance to question her. I don't want to puncture Mom's well-maintained veneer. It pains me that she is losing her verve, so I pretend this isn't so. The more passive Mom becomes, the more I hold back. *Don't upset the apple cart.*

We tiptoe past an untouchable myth. Mom insists that Dad is "perfect" when they travel. Away from 2 Laurel he is instantly happy. He becomes the cheerful, playful person she married when they were both only twenty-one. They call each other "Poopie" again and laugh; therefore he can't be an alcoholic. And yet, I remind myself, they always come home, and the furies descend.

I take a different tack and start analyzing Dad's upbringing. His conception was an accident, his birth an anticlimax. Nana liked to recall how much she'd wept that Dad wasn't a girl, especially since he was her "spit and image." Studio portraits show Dad at the age of three sporting a blond Dutch cut and immaculate Little Lord Fauntleroy suits. His parents were happy to hand him and his brother Bobby to nannies to be raised. Stories abound of how viciously they teased each other, but they were never separated or corrected.

Temper tantrums were accepted as a clan trademark. On the tennis court at Tahoe I remember Stanley habitually swearing and hurling his tennis racket to the ground as everyone looked on impassively. Back then, Dad's outbursts seemed mild in comparison.

"The family put up with such crazy behavior," I say to Mom. "Why wasn't anyone in charge?"

"His parents were completely unpsychological," says Mom. "No one had the tools back then. If only he would see a therapist again."

"Probably the same thing would happen," says Peter. "His appointments with Dr. B became joke sessions over lunch."

"There's nothing Henry likes to do," says Mom. "He has no interests."

"He likes to cook," I say.

"No, I mean out of the house. I want him out."

And this is where our talk grinds to a halt. Neither Mom nor Dad will budge from 2 Laurel, or, as Peter calls it, "Too Laurel." We all know the drill. The game isn't meant to change. *I'm It. You're It. Olly, olly, oxen free.*

The Temple Raffle

*B*ennie Blume, the furrier, is beside himself with excitement. It is time for the annual temple raffle, and he is dying to win a prize. To boost his chances he buys $10,000 worth of raffle tickets.

The drawing begins. Grunsveld, president of Beth Am Congregation, spins the raffle drum and announces, "Third prize, a gold-plated Cadillac convertible with white patent leather seats and spoke wheels, goes to . . ."

The drum slows to a stop. Grunsveld reaches in and pulls out the winning ticket stub. He puts on his bifocals and squints at the name, "Rabinowitz! Sy Rabinowitz. Mazel tov!"

Everyone ooohs and ahhhs. Bennie Blume is beginning to sweat. Only two more prizes to go.

Grunsveld spins the raffle drum for second prize: "A chocolate cake with buttercream frosting baked by the rabbi's wife!"

Grunsveld draws another ticket stub, turns it over, readjusts his glasses, and announces, "The cake goes to Bennie Blume!"

"Fuck the rabbi's wife!" shouts Bennie Blume.

"No," says Grunsveld, "that's first prize!"

Yankee Doodle Dandy

1944–1945

Dad grows misty when he remembers World War II.

"It was the only independence I ever had," he says.

The navy saved Dad from the tedium of working at D. N. & E. and gave him his first employment outside the family. Confinement on board the USS *Audubon*, an attack transport, with the Sixth Fleet in the far Pacific was freedom for Dad. A self-proclaimed "devout coward," he cheerfully memorized and enforced navy rules, embraced routine, and stayed away from combat on his supply ship.

While Dad was overseas, Mom, newborn Peter, and I moved to Gaggy's house in San Francisco. She lived in a hulking, brown, three-storied Victorian mansion with turrets and stained-glass windows. It darkened the corner of Clay and Buchanan streets opposite what was then Stanford Hospital. The house was set apart from the street by a spiky, wrought-iron fence and rolling lawns. A frowsy palm tree overshadowed the entry. Its big, flat fronds sighed and slapped against the house in the wind.

Gaggy was known as "the widow of Clay Street." When John I. Walter died in 1930, she donned "widow's weeds" and wore only black for nearly two decades. By the time we came to live with her, my oldest cousin, Margot, had introduced her to lipstick, a bright, Minnie Mouse red.

After breakfast in bed, Gaggy would come downstairs in a tailored black dress, pearls, and high heels. She dusted her face with white powder that clung to the downy fuzz on her cheeks. Her long white hair was always piled softly on her head like a meringue. She had a graceful, long neck and sad, blue eyes with soft hooded lids that veiled her thoughts. She reminded me of the black swan at the Palace of Fine Arts pond, where she took me on sunny afternoons to feed the ducks. The swan floated in her own regal orbit, proud and alone—the only one without a mate, the one all the others followed.

Gaggy would give menus and instructions for the day written in purple ink to her help. Then she retired to her bookbindery to work. Sometimes I was permitted to be there if I was quiet. I would play under one of the huge work tables, spinning Venetian glass paperweights or compressing one of her giant sea sponges, then letting it pop back into shape. During Sunday night dinners my older cousins and I would sneak into the bindery to play in the vertical book press. Its crank was like a steering wheel in a car. We took turns inserting our torsos and seeing how much pressure we could endure.

My most intimate moments alone with Gaggy took place upstairs in her long, white-tiled bathroom, where she bathed each evening before dinner. She floated in a brimming, claw-footed bathtub. One of her own round, hand-crocheted washcloths covered her convex breast-bone and jelly-bean nipples. She lay there until the water was completely still.

After her bath and before her martini, Gaggy dressed in a hostess gown, then lit a candle beside John I. Walter's picture. It stood on a bedside table in a leather double frame that displayed his last love letter to her: "If I should die tomorrow, I love you for your great blue eyes" and for her many other attributes. Gaggy performed this solemn ritual every night for the forty-two years she lived on without him. The steadfastness of her love seemed to me as solid as the lead weights that flattened the books in her bindery.

At the other end of the hall was a cozy sitting room with an upright piano. Gaggy would play and sing, "I Went to the Animal Fair" and "Pop Goes the Weasel." Then we'd snuggle together in her overstuffed armchair while she had her drink, brooded silently, and occasionally told stories of her house.

It had survived the 1906 earthquake. During the fire that followed, the Red Cross set up a relief station on the lawn to feed and house the firemen. She and her younger sister, Pearl, had grown up in the house and had lived there for two years after marrying the Walter brothers, John I. and Edgar. Tragically, Pearl died at twenty-eight of pernicious anemia. Much too soon after, Pearl's husband, Edgar, a sculptor, married his model, Betty. Gaggy never allowed him back in the house. Her hatred was as steadfast as her love.

Gaggy would gaze out through the venetian blinds to Stanford Hospital across the street and remember other deaths. Her first born, and only son, John Walter, died at home of pneumonia in 1919 at the age of eleven. In 1930 her husband died in their four-poster after a long kidney illness. It seemed that all the people Gaggy had loved the most had died.

Sometimes she would sing:

Oh, when I die, don't bury me at all.

Just pickle my bones in alcohol.
Lay a bottle of booze at my head and feet.
That way I'll know my bones will keep.

Then she would hug me tightly and say, "I have a secret to tell you: I love you!"

I couldn't imagine anyone I loved dying. Despite the stories, I felt safe living in Gaggy's house. It was the embodiment of family. It had become a house of inter-marriage for the next generation, too. In 1929 Nell Walter had married Stanley Sinton. In 1938, "another Sinton got into hot Walter," as the saying went, and my parents, Carol Walter and Henry Sinton, married at home. It was the fifth time in two generations that brothers from one family had married sisters of another. I assumed this happened in all families.

It gave me great comfort when I was a child to count my relatives as I fell asleep at night. I imagined which ones would adopt Peter and me if we were suddenly orphaned. This anxiety was probably set off by Mom and Dad's six-week absences when they took pleasure trips abroad. They left us in the care of warm-hearted and conscientious helpers, but I must have worried that they wouldn't come back.

At the top of my list were Auntie Nell and Uncle Stanley because both were blood relatives. Next in line were the two who had strayed from the fold and married outsiders: Uncle Bobby and Auntie Joan, Auntie Marge and Uncle Paul. Each of these couples had three children, so whichever family took us in would offer the added excitement of cousins.

Gaggy's age disqualified her as a permanent guardian,

I reasoned, and to be fair I applied this same standard to Dad's parents, Stanley (Poppa) and Edna (Nana) Sinton.

It would not have been nice to admit that I had favorites, though I quietly did. The scales tilted most decidedly in Gaggy's direction. Besides living with her for nearly two years during the War and attending Sunday dinners, I also spent all of July and August with her at Walter Lodge at Rampart on the Truckee River near Lake Tahoe.

It was at Rampart in 1929 that Dad, then twelve, met Mom. The Sintons and Walters were already inter-related old friends, and Nell and Stanley were soon to be engaged. During this visit Dad first heard John I. Walter read aloud from Milt Gross's "Nize Baby." The slapstick stories were written in imitation of a thick Yiddish accent that made my grandfather cry with laughter:

> Oohoo, nize baby, itt opp all de Cheeken Zoop so mamma'll gonna tell you a Ferry-Tail from Keeng Mitas. Wance oppon a time was a werry, werry reech Keeng from de name from Keeng Mitas. Sotch a welt wot he hed!—wot it would make J. P. Morgan witt Hanry Fudd witt Joh D. Rock-efeller dey should look like puppers. (Nize baby, take anodder spoon cheeken zoop—)

John Walter's paroxysms made a huge impression on Dad. He yearned to be the one to kill people with laughter. It is no surprise that he fell willingly into the Walter orbit and became the court jester.

By comparison, Nana and Poppa exerted no patri-archal force. They were generous and rich and sociable. Nana played canasta and mahjong with her friends, and Poppa played golf and hunted duck with his. They weren't much interested in us but liked having children around as background music. We were included in feasts at their elegant apartment, which occupied the whole tenth floor of a Russian Hill high-rise where Green Street dead-ended. We spun ourselves dizzy on the big automobile turntable in the basement garage.

At the linen-draped dining-room table we were seated according to age among our Sinton cousins, far from Nana and Poppa. Their warm, exuberant French helpers made all of us feel special and beloved, and I spent much more time chatting with Angele, Louise, and Henri than I did with Nana and Poppa.

All my grandparents' live-in help appeared to serve life sentences without parole or complaint. At Gaggy's their only day off each week, Thursday, left us feeling bereft. The house was dark and cavernous without them. Their presence insulated us and made me feel that all was right in the world. I could count on the hubbub in the pantry with its bright blue linoleum floor and the buttery smell of Fong's freshly baked ladyfingers. In the lull between meals I climbed the narrow back stairs to the maids' sunny bedrooms in the attic, with its brown linoleum floors and toasty scent of steam ironing. Agatha told stories of her family in France and showed me pictures of her daughter, Juliette, and grandson. Mary saved postcards from her relatives in snowy Denmark. Fong had a daughter, Amy, who visited him in his small, spare room, converted from a hayloft in a detached carriage house that once kept horses. I never questioned why the help didn't live with their own families. I assumed we were their family first. The entitlement implicit in this assumption appalls me now, but we were ignorant of it then.

Dad wrote to Mom every day during his year overseas—his way of letting her know his precise location. Of course this was forbidden during wartime, but Dad, in a moment of devious genius, invented a secret code for pinpointing the latitude and longitude of his ship.

"Not even the Japanese could crack it!" he often tells me with relish. "At the top of every letter I wrote the date. If the number appeared to the right of the month—July 10, for example—it meant east longitude. But if I wrote '10 July,' it meant west longitude. Then I wrote the time, navy style, to indicate the degree of longitude. So 'July 10, 16:00' meant 160 degrees east longitude.

"The first paragraph told latitude. A question meant northern latitude; a statement meant southern. Everyone in the family had a different number corresponding to their name. Gaggy was 2. Your mother was 3. You were 4. Peter was 5. Punch [our dog] was 6, so if I wrote 'I miss Pat and Peter and Punch,' I was indicating that I was 15 degrees south. If I asked, 'How are Pat and Peter?,' I'd be 9 degrees north."

Returning from war to the family fold was a mixed blessing for Dad. Back home his choice was to revert to being Heinie, The Little Fella, in his family of origin or submit to Gaggy's ironclad matriarchy.

"I chose the easy way," he would later tell me. "You do what your family expects of you."

Lacking a more ambitious vision for his life, Dad cheerfully reclaimed his role as jester. No one came close to filling that spot. All his life Dad told jokes to win love and absolution. First thing each day he would go to the office with a new or improved story to make Stanley laugh.

Grand Opening

Walgreens is opening a new superstore on the corner of First and Mission. A hundred prizes have been promised. The prize for the first in line is a thirty-two-inch color TV. A huge crowd gathers hours before the 9 AM opening. The line stretches around the block, and the crowd is very eager and restless.

At 8:50 a little schmendrick in a plaid suit shows up and starts pushing his way to the front of the line. A big muscle man in a T-shirt and jeans picks him up by the lapels of his jacket and throws him into the street.

The little schmendrick picks himself up and tries again. This time two men in business suits shove him back down the sidewalk and into the street.

One more time the little schmendrick gets up, brushes some schmutz off his pants, and pushes his way back to the head of the line.

"So help me God," he says, "if you lay one more hand on me, I won't open the store!"

The Dentex Salesman

Proctor and Gamble is putting out a new toothpaste, Dentex. It is a flop everywhere except in one region near Schenectady, New York, where Epstein is selling it hand over fist. The directors decide to have a national meeting for their entire sales force, and they invite Epstein to speak.

Little Epstein goes to the front of the lecture hall and sets up his display.

"First, put a card table near the entrance of the supermarket. Then put out toothbrushes, paper cups, and a pitcher of water. Give the shoppers a free toothbrush if they sample Dentex. Dip the toothbrush in a little water, squeeze on the Dentex, and watch them start brushing. As soon as they spit it out and say, "This tastes like shit!" you tell 'em, "See, already it's working!"

Sadie Schwartz in Miami Beach

Young Sadie Schwartz is married to Abe, a very successful trader on Wall Street, very rich. Come February they are going to Miami Beach, but things are huckle-de-buck in the market. Abe decides he has to stay home and work, so Sadie goes without him.

She is very young and absolutely gorgeous. She checks into the Fountainebleau Hotel and meets this beautiful, strong bellhop, handsome like Harry Belafonte and healthy like a horse. They start having this marvelous affair. She's never had it like this with Abe.

One day Sadie decides it's time for her annual pap smear. She asks the concierge if there are any good gynecologists in Miami Beach.

"The best!" he says. "I'll get you an appointment with Dr. Feldman."

Next day Sadie goes to the doctor. He puts in the speculum and takes a look.

"I gotta tell you," he says, "I've been in this business forty-two years and never have I seen such a clean vagina."

"It ought to be," says Sadie. "The shvartzer comes twice a week."

Hickory, Dickory, Dock

1950s

Gaggy's Victorian mansion is long gone, razed in the 1950s after William Wurster designed and built her a modern showcase at the dead end of Larkin Street. Today, three-story apartment cubicles occupy the corner lot where Gaggy's huge house and rolling lawns once presided. Thirty-four separate addresses supplant her single one at 2299 Clay Street.

A new era was dawning. First to go was Gaggy's chauffeur and the big black Chrysler limousine. She got a black Studebaker instead, one of those early '50s models that looked the same front and back. When Gaggy drove, you couldn't tell if it was coming or going.

But Gaggy never wavered. She managed a decade of dislocations with the steely assurance and precision of a watchmaker. From my pre-adolescent perspective, events still conformed to her will. Sit-down dinners every other Sunday night continued as they had on Clay Street and stabilized the school year. Attendance at Rampart during July and August anchored the summers.

A retinue of six or seven white-uniformed helpers kept Walter Lodge running in Edwardian style. When all of Gaggy's immediate family were present, we numbered fifteen. The addition of close friends and other relatives often increased that to twenty-five and more. The help ate together in a little kitchen-dining room in the Big House. Children under twelve ate in the Little House with their nannies. Then we graduated to eating with the grown-ups in the Big House. Since Peter and I were the youngest, we got to advance together when I turned twelve. After dinner the adults and children all played charades.

Gaggy presiding over family.   Photo by Ann Rosener, 1950

Gaggy ordered fresh produce from Lorenzini Brothers in San Francisco. A shipment arrived each week by Railway Express. To collect it, my cousins and I rode to Tahoe City in the back of an old black pickup driven by a hired college boy. We also got daily groceries from the Village Store, as well as San Francisco newspapers and mail from the post office.

In 1953 I was allowed to leave Rampart for two weeks to join some of my school friends at Camp Sugar Pine, a no-frills Girl Scout camp in the sun-baked Sierra foothills in Calaveras County. Mom and Dad drove me from Tahoe in Dad's dark-green Cadillac convertible with tan leather seats. The top was down, and it was a cloudless, hot day.

Camp Sugar Pine had no lake, no stream, no swimming pool. There were no cabins, just a lot of lodgepole pines that became rooms once we lashed sturdy sticks between them. We hung our towels and clothes from these poles. Then we leveled the dusty ground under them with our bare hands and piled pine needles at least six inches thick to make mattresses on which to place our sleeping bags. Once we got set up, there was nothing to do except wait for our periods to start.

Most girls had a pubic hair or two, and some had the beginnings of breasts. The envied few with well-developed bosoms had already menstruated and came to camp equipped with Kotex and an elastic belt. When my best friend, Nancy, got her first period at camp, a pamphlet, "Growing Up and Liking It," mysteriously appeared on her sleeping bag. One insecure girl was stupid enough to pretend she had started, too, but she was quickly ratted out. The tap of a hand mid-back revealed the absence of a bra, considered to be a prerequisite for menstruation.

I had inherited a training bra from my precocious friend, Margie Kahn, who'd outgrown it. I'd sewn a few tucks in the cups to get them to conform to my flat chest, then modeled my creation for Mom and Dad.

"A training bra?" asked Dad. "What are you training them to do?"

"To grow."

I knew better than to risk ridicule by bringing my training bra to camp, but I prayed nightly for the miracle of breasts.

Camp Sugar Pine boasted no buildings other than a shower house and a kitchen with an open-air dining platform with long picnic tables and benches. We sat for hours after dinner singing. We sang rounds of "White Coral Bells" and "Hay, Ho, Nobody Home." We harmonized "Little Shepherd Boy" and "Swinging Along the Open Road." We even tackled dirges like "Rushes and Roars the Wide Dnieper" under the vigorous conducting of Hermit Thrush. All the counselors were older women who took the names of local critters. Nuthatch taught arts and crafts. Beetle knew first aid.

Three days before the camp session ended, my prayers were answered. I woke up with a tender swelling under my right nipple. It felt like a small button beneath the skin. I touched it often. It was there the next morning and the next—a breast bud! I could hardly wait for Mom and Dad to arrive from Tahoe to tell them my news.

I was packed and ready to go when they showed up on time. I introduced them to Gopher, the head counselor.

"Howdy, Miss Gopher," said Dad in a goofy accent. "Glad to meetcha!"

I would have died of embarrassment if I hadn't been trying so hard to contain my secret. We drove off. After a mile or two, I told Dad to stop the car and follow me. I had something to show them. I got out of the car and ran toward a cluster of trees away from the highway.

"Come. Look!" I said, lifting my tee shirt.

"Oh, Patchy, that's quite a bee sting," said Dad.

My absorption in my own pubescence and need for popularity made me oblivious to the changes taking place in my family. I overheard Dad rumbling about leaving D.N. & E. and getting a commercial real estate license, but didn't consider the impact this would have. I didn't comment on Mom's swift progress as a weaver, nor did I join discussions of Peter's high school options. I was on the girl track at Burke's, a K–12 girls' school. He was on the boy track, destined to go from Town School for Boys to Lick and ultimately to Menlo. None of the private schools were co-ed in those days.

I did tune in to the dinner-table talk when pristine Squaw Valley was chosen as the site for the 1960 Olympics. Tobacco-chewing, hunchbacked Bud Jones and his stable of riding horses had already been forced out of the lush meadow that was to become a vast parking lot. Gaggy feared that the quiet bucolic nature of the Truckee River would be next to go. Ever since the historic snowfall in the winter of 1951, which caused windows, porches, and walls to collapse, the upkeep of Rampart had become more difficult. The plumbing had always been primitive. Hot water depended on keeping a wood fire going in a brick kiln up the hill above the guest cabins, where water was piped from an icy mountain spring.

No one in the family wanted to take on the challenge of running Rampart. Gaggy had set too high a standard. Mom and Dad's generation just wanted out, and mine wasn't ready to step up. Dad, now a newly licensed realtor, helped Gaggy analyze the choices. She rejected the commercial option of winterizing the houses and renting to skiers and put Rampart on the market.

During this unsettled decade, Poppa received a diagnosis of pancreatic cancer. He often came to sit in the afternoon sun in our garden. He appeared to be losing weight and wanted to talk alone with Mom. With relief, I retreated to my room to write letters to my boyfriend and never wondered how Poppa's illness might be affecting Dad. Dad allowed himself to display pride and anger but not sadness or disappointment.

In 1954 Poppa died. I learned only recently from my cousin Douglas that Dad had been excluded from the deathbed gathering. When he arrived to see Poppa one last time, Stanley and Bobby had turned him away at the hospital room door, supposedly on Poppa's orders.

"Don't let Heinie in. He irritates me."

The pain of this rejection must have endured for the rest of Dad's life. The fact that Dad never told me indicates the depth of his hurt.

How a Woman Is Like the Continents

Between the ages of sixteen and eighteen, a woman is like Africa, virgin and unexplored.

Between the ages of nineteen and thirty-five, she is like Asia, hot and exotic.

Between the ages of thirty-six and forty-five, she is like America, fully explored, breathtakingly beautiful, and free with her resources.

Between the ages of forty-six and fifty-six she is like Europe, mature, cultivated, full of points of interest.

After fifty-six, she is like Australia: everybody knows it's down there, but nobody wants to go.

Humpty Dumpty

1960–1990

During my college years, Mom and Dad shed helpers, from two to one to none, and blossomed into jubilant domestics. Liberated from Tahoe, they bought a country house of their own, which doubled their chores. They were nesters through and through, no matter that the nest was empty except for them and their dog. They were the perfect au pair: Dad, the inventive fix-it man, driver, and barbecue chef, and Mom, the tireless gardener and gourmet cook. Her labor-intensive hors d'oeuvres were not intended to satisfy hungry children. We dubbed her the inventor of "Cuisine Miser."

Photo by Kate Kline May, 1994

Growing old was not for them, as if it were an option. Refusing help proved that they were still young and capable. Mom became such a compulsive domestic worker that washing dishes was her badge of honor. She batted away unwelcome assistance saying, "I can do it! You make me feel incompetent."

Mom and Dad's thirty years of solo domestic servitude away from the city brought pleasure and stability. I think they were happiest together when they were enclosed in the car, like astronauts in a space capsule, hurtling passively toward a fresh destination.

They needed to escape. In 1968 the bombshell of Nell and Stanley's divorce shook the family. None of our relatives had ever divorced. Gaggy's world was shattered. She felt personally betrayed because she depended on Stanley to be both her financial advisor and D. N. & E.'s courtly heir. Gaggy unleashed her quivering fury against Stanley by directing it to the nearest proxy, Dad.

"Your brother is one hell of a sonofabitch!"

Dad weathered the verbal abuse stoically. He knew it would be futile to try to defend Stanley. Gaggy's attacks cemented Dad's brotherly bonds and made life more difficult for Mom, too. Both of them were trapped. Running away to the country together every weekend was a salvation that kept their marriage going.

Dad, the self-proclaimed best driver in the world, had a sense of direction as flawless as his 20/20 vision. He knew every shortcut and scenic two-lane road. He took Mom exploring on all the back roads of Marin and Sonoma counties. As long as Dad could drive, he and Mom would be together and dodge old age.

Then, in 1990, out of nowhere, came the diagnosis of macular degeneration.

Dad was losing his eyesight in both eyes—irreversibly, irretrievably. He could never—would never—accept it. Hell-bent on fury, Dad cursed fate and marshaled his iron will.

Over many a vodka, he plotted his next moves and sharpened his defiance. He repelled our pleas to stop driving, until one evening in the spring of 1997: as he was driving home from downtown, the setting sun so blinded him that he almost hit a dog. That near-miss shocked him enough to give up driving forever.

Now Dad would have to depend on others. They would have to do things exactly as he did, *comme il faut.* His way was the only way. As his eyesight and hearing deserted him, other senses came to the fore. He became hypervigilant and acutely aware of everything going on around him. He replayed old memories, especially the painful ones.

"I have the opposite of Alzheimer's," he said. "I can't forget a fuckin' thing!"

The Tale of Mrs. Van Smythe

Poor Mrs. Van Smythe goes to see her doctor because lately she's been having the most terrible bouts of flatulence.

"Such huge volume, Doctor, but, fortunately, no odor or sound. However with ballet season starting—we have seats in center orchestra—I am so afraid of embarrassing myself."

"Of course, Mrs. Van Smythe. I understand completely," says the doctor. "Here, let me give you some pills which should help. Come back in two weeks, and let me know how you are doing."

Two weeks later Mrs. Van Smythe returns.

"Oh, Doctor, it's ever so much worse. I still have great quantities of gas, but now it is accompanied by an extremely foul odor. Fortunately there is no sound."

"Oh, that is grand, Mrs. Van Smythe. I am so glad to hear that. The prescription has cleared your sinuses. Now, this week we will work on your hearing."

Fe, Fi, Fo, Fum

1965

I met Ron on a double blind date camping trip over Labor Day weekend in September 1965. Our adventure started on the doorstep of my roommate's family house in San Francisco. I tugged open the heavy front door, and there he stood—tall, thin, and eager. His kind, green eyes greeted mine. He was twenty-two and a second-year medical student at Stanford. I was twenty-four and teaching history at Berkeley High. We were both struck by an undeniable familiarity, as if we had already known each other. Our paths had almost crossed at Harvard, but the sense of connection went much deeper.

"Why don't you come in my car with me?" Ron suggested. "I want to stop by Simon Brothers to buy beverages for the weekend."

"Oh," I laughed, "my parents and grandparents shop there all the time."

Ron had known Jeff Simon since kindergarten, and he wanted to say hello to Jeff's father, Lucien.

When Ron and I walked into the store together, Lucien raced over with tears in his eyes.

"This was meant to be! Oh, this was meant to be," he kept repeating as he hugged us to his chest and plied us with samples of dill pickles and lox and fine chocolates. On our way back to the car Ron said, "I guess we're married now."

Ron was everything my family wasn't. He was a penniless immigrant who worked hard for everything he got. His German Jewish parents met in 1934 while fleeing Hitler. They settled in Bombay, where Ron's maternal grandfather had an import business selling Singer sewing machines. Ron was born in Bombay and sailed to California with his family when he was four. We grew up in different worlds within San Francisco. He went to public schools and swam at the city's Sutro Baths. I went to private schools and swam in a relative's private pool in Atherton. I wasn't allowed to swim at Sutro because of the threat of polio.

Ron and I spent every weekend together after that first date. While hiking the Steep Ravine Trail in Marin three weeks after we'd met, Ron turned to me and said, "You're just the kind of person I want to marry!"

I felt the same way about him. He was the first person I'd ever imagined marrying, but as I parsed his blurted confession, I realized that it wasn't a proposal. Was I just a category of person, or was I *the* person?

In the months that followed, Ron retreated from the topic, and I tried to downplay my growing concern. If talk of marriage ever did come up, Ron headed for the nearest exit: "I'm much too young. I can't possibly think about marriage until I know what kind of a doctor I'm going to be."

What difference would it make, I asked, if he were to choose ophthalmology or pediatrics, radiology or internal medicine? Clearly, he was panicking, and so was I. By March I needed to decide whether to renew my contract at Berkeley High. Ron wanted me to live with him, but I needed more of a commitment.

In April Dad began rumbling to me that Ron "should shit or get off the pot." He and Mom loved Ron and knew I did, too. I met them for a bon voyage dinner the night before they were to leave for a month in Italy. At the end of the meal, Dad said, "If that boy hasn't proposed by the time I get back, I'm going to have words with him."

This threat was so unthinkable that I couldn't react. Of all Dad's utterances, this one alarmed me most. I was certain he would drive Ron away. As I had done so many times before, I tried to tamp down Dad's words and pretend to be unmoved. Nothing Dad said was going to affect me.

A couple of weeks later, after another wonderful weekend together, Ron phoned as he always did on Sunday night to be sure I'd gotten home safely. While we were talking, he mentioned that Ray and Priscilla, a couple we hardly knew and didn't particularly like, were engaged.

Something in me snapped.

"That's the stupidest thing I've ever heard!" I said. "They're not the ones who should be getting married. We should."

"Oh dear," said Ron. "I'd better drive up. We need to talk."

I told him no, I had to prepare for my classes. Ron offered to come the next evening, but I was going out on a blind date in the city. Uncle Stanley had a Swiss businessman in tow, and in light of Ron's skittishness about commitment, I'd decided to get back in circulation.

"Then I'll come up after your date."

We agreed to meet at 2 Laurel since my parents were still in Italy. I told him where to find the secret key.

When I entered the house after my date, a note from Ron was on the bottom stair. A torn scrap of paper with my name and phone number, which he'd carried in his wallet ever since our first date, was scotch-taped to a note that read: "This is how it all began. To find out what happens next, climb the stairs and ask the man with the mango stains on his shirt."

We got married at 2 Laurel on a sweltering July 24, 1966. In the middle of dinner shrieks of laughter exploded from our grandmothers, who were seated together and meeting for the first time. The party fell silent as everyone turned to watch the whooping women. Finally, one of them caught her breath long enough to announce that Ron's great uncle, Alphonse Blum, had been married to my grandmother's first cousin, Emma Bing, back in Freiburg, Germany. Our families were already connected.

The Cow from Minsk

In a shtetl in Russia the only cow has grown too old to give milk. The villagers are desperate for a new young one to breed with their bull. They send Mordecai the herder to search the neighboring shtetls. He has to go all the way to Minsk to find a good cow.

The new cow is young and beautiful—black and white with a shiny pink nose. All the villagers gather to watch Mordecai lead the bull to her pasture. The bull is very excited to see such a fine cow. He paws the ground and snorts as he approaches her, but the cow darts this way and that, always twirling away any time the bull gets close.

Mordecai and the villagers decide to wait a day and try again. But the next day and the next, the same thing happens. No matter how the bull approaches, the cow manages to move away. If he approaches from the front, she moves back. If he approaches from the back, she runs forward and spins around to face him.

The villagers are very worried and need milk badly, so they call in the wise rabbi. The rabbi comes to the pasture to see for himself, and, sure enough, it is just as the villagers described. The bull charges eagerly into the pasture with his tail raised. The cow backs away. She turns this way and that, always facing the bull to keep him away from her hindquarters. After the bull makes many attempts to approach her, the cow lies down with a loud groan in a corner of the pasture and presses her haunches against the fence.

The rabbi watches intently and strokes his beard. "Tell me," he asks, "is this cow from Minsk?"

"Yes!" say the villagers. "You are a wise rabbi. How did you know?"

"My wife is from Minsk."

Bobby's Funeral

June 6, 1997

Uncle Bobby's funeral is an affair of state. He is the last of our uncles, the self-appointed patriarch. For two years Dad has seen this day coming, as Bobby declined from slow, irreversible lung fibrosis. Dad had never been alive a day without him. He glommed onto Bobby like a tick, no matter how mercilessly he teased and taunted.

I sit next to my brother, Peter, at funerals. He brings extra Kleenex. When the cantor sings her first sad, liquid notes, Peter's big, warm bulk begins to shake. I sidle closer, and we clutch hands the way we did when we tried to watch *Pinocchio* or *Bambi* together fifty years ago.

We are sitting in the front section of the synagogue, reserved for family. Our enduring spouses, Bev and Ron, flank us. In the next row, directly in front of me, sit Mom and Dad. I scan our clan, pleased to see cousins all around. When we get together, we become children again, but now, seated in temple, we are the fading ones with the gray hair and respectable suits. Our handsome, grown children eclipse us. They look huge, colorful, glorious!

Mom and Dad look small, drab, and spent. Their clothes don't fit quite right and have the air of hand-me-downs, worn too many times in better days. Mom's knit suit, a little too lavender for somber Temple Emanu-El, droops from her tiny shoulders. The label of her blouse is sticking up. I tuck it back in. She looks at her wristwatch, and I know she is impatient for the service to begin and be done because she has a hair appointment at twelve thirty, which she will not change. Her weekly appointment is inviolable. Nothing, not death nor sickness nor war nor natural disaster, will keep her from it.

Doing her own hair is about the only thing Mom can't manage. She can spin, knit, weave, loop rugs, and construct baskets, wall hangings, and collages, but she cannot wash her own hair. It is fine, like a baby's, and requires a body wave and hair spray to be "right." Today it is in need of a master's touch. The crown and sides have flattened, and the wave on top is a bit askew. But the most amazing thing about my mother's hair is that it refuses to turn gray. She has never dyed it. It is permanently, eternally brown. She cannot understand why mine, at fifty-six, is white.

Dad, thank God, has gotten dressed, not as impeccably as he used to but better than usual. In college pictures he could have been a Great Gatsby stand-in: cocky in white bucks, crisp shirt and blazer, and spotless, well-fitted slacks. He was so Ivy League, such a Yalie, almost too blond and beautiful to be a guy. He never owned a pair of jeans. To this day his motto is, "Dress British. Think Yiddish."

He insists he still has magnificent taste, even though he refuses to change clothes for a week at a time. He wears the same tattered, blue Shetland sweater, grease-stained trousers, and scuffed, oversized, brown oxfords that have never known a shine. I don't know if this is a result of his worsening macular degeneration or a form of warfare against Mom, who chooses not to get involved except for uttering bitter, disparaging comments. "Look at him—he's a sight." Yet she seems not to see the spots on her own clothes, and as her late-in-life thrift intensifies, she shuns the dry cleaners at all cost.

For Bobby's funeral Dad has managed to dress up in one of his finest gabardine J. Press suits. He has chosen an exquisite pinstripe shirt ("from Savile Row, natch") and a silk paisley tie ("Old Madder, the best"). His white hair is washed and carefully parted. He smoothes it down with his hand and fiddles with his hearing aid. I wonder if he is turning it off, as he often does in large, echoing surroundings.

Temple is not a place he likes to be, especially not in Bobby's shadow. Dad often grumbled that Bobby had become a "Super Jew" in the aftermath of the Holocaust. As if to atone for his youthful insensitivity and lack of Jewish identity, Bobby became the darling of San Francisco Jewry and flourished as president of and star fundraiser for the Jewish Community Federation.

"You'd think he'd been struck by lightning," Dad once complained to me. "It was as if he'd invented it. And he took all the honors."

Dad remained a secular Jew, drawn to Jewish humor, folk wisdom, and ethics but untouched by ritual and pedagogy. He never shared his family's repressed anti-Semitism, which expressed itself in a "don't ask, don't tell" stance toward Judaism. Their childhood years spent in Beverly, Massachusetts, a posh Boston suburb, taught them to pass into the beautiful WASP world. The brothers succeeded and got as far as Yale.

There, Dad and Bobby's paths diverged. In Dad's words, Bobby became a "goy chaser," eager to shed any Jewish trappings, while Dad became fast friends with his Jewish roommate, Herb Salzman. He often visited Herb's

Yiddish-speaking family in New York. Mama Salzman called Dad Herschel and took him to their conservative temple. Dad didn't care much for the "mumbo jumbo," but he felt as though he'd landed in the middle of a Milt Gross story. Dad reveled in their Jewish identity and *weltschmerz*, which his own German Jewish family played down, and he used it to endear himself as the irreverent Jewish joke teller.

Funerals, even less loaded ones, usually make Mom and Dad cross; there have been far too many lately. Their generation has all but deserted them. It is Mom and Dad's style to quickly turn sad into mad, but today they are too sad to be cross.

Clare, a granddaughter, is speaking:

Poppop, as we grandchildren called him, was one of the few people I've known who loved being old. When I was little, he would brag to me about his age as evidenced by the inelasticity of his skin. He would grab my inexperienced hand, pinch a mound of flesh, and quickly release—mirroring these gestures on his own hand to illustrate the difference between age and youth. We would both marvel at the outcome of the experiment: my skin popping back into place immediately, his skin settling slowly and patiently into his hand. For me, this patient settling of skin and his own curiosity about the process stands as an image of his grace in illness and finally death.

Peter's grip on my hand tightens excruciatingly. A great, silent sob shudders through him. Bobby was his special protector and ally, quick to defend him from Dad's unfair assaults—a surrogate father. Tears splash down Peter's cheeks and soak into the shoulder pads of his jacket or land on my skirt. Oh, to have a father, patriarchal and tender, who could grow old with grace! Oh, to be able to remember a sweet moment, to feel a loving loss!

Peter leans into me, moans into my ear, "What're we going to do? Oh, what're we going to do?" and I know he means what are we going to do when Dad dies, and it's our turn. What do we do with a father who has forsaken his own brilliant promise and who has caught us in his misery?

Young Shapiro Goes to Harvard

Such a brilliant boy is young Shapiro that he gets accepted to Harvard at the age of twelve. This is so unusual that President Conant has invited the boy and his parents, Max and Rachel, to come to Cambridge for a private interview the day before fall semester starts.

Max Shapiro, bursting with pride, shakes hands with President Conant and says, "President Conant, I want my son should be 100 percent Yankee Doodle boy. I want him to speak like you, not me."

"In that case, Mr. Shapiro," says President Conant in perfect King's English, "to lose his accent and to acquire proper intonation and syntax, there must be no contact, none whatsoever, between you and your son from now until graduation day four years hence. I will see to it that he has employment and housing over the holidays and summers, but he may not speak to either of you over the phone, nor may he visit."

"You know best," says Max. "We will miss him, but we will do whatever you say."

After four long years Max and Rachel return to Cambridge on graduation day. Before the ceremony they have been summoned to meet with President Conant in his office to find out how their boy has turned out.

President Conant hears them coming down the hall and rushes out of his office to greet them.

"Mr. Shapiro! Oy, is that a boy!"

Nepenthe[*]

June 1997

I am talking to two dogs on a shady patch of lawn near Highway 1 in Big Sur. I came to this spot just beyond the Nepenthe Restaurant parking lot, wanting to give the dogs a breather. They'd been locked in the car all through lunch, but sitting here I realize I'm the one in need. I've brought Mom and Dad away for three days to lift their spirits after Bobby's funeral, and I'm succumbing to the kind of fatigue I haven't felt since my own children were toddlers.

How has it come to this? Perhaps I should have heeded Dean Sherman's stark warning to me thirty-six years ago when she reigned as dean of Radcliffe College. I had phoned her from San Francisco during summer vacation after my sophomore year to tell her that I was thinking of remaining in California and taking courses at U.C. Berkeley.

After a long, icy pause, Dean Sherman said, "You are throwing your life away."

And click! The line went dead. I was out of Radcliffe with no questions asked, no other options explored. In one rash, unblinking second, I had thrown my life away!

---

[*] Nepenthe is something that induces forgetfulness of grief or easing pain and also a legendary drug of ancient times used as a remedy for sorrow.

We've eaten an early lunch, barely two hours after finishing breakfast. Their urgency about eating intensifies with age. Even with scones still in our stomachs and no one else in the restaurant, there was the trembling rush to procure a table, menus, and drinks all in the same instant, the anxious wait for the food, the momentary relief when both the waitress and the hamburgers measured up, and then the plotting where to eat our next meal. At this rate we will be ready for dinner at three, but that is unthinkable. They are too cosmopolitan to eat before seven. We will fill in by having a tour of Post Ranch, tea in Carmel, and baths before dinner.

Sweetie, their corgi-"terror" mix, is straining to get away and rejoin her people in the Nepenthe gift shop. Lizzie, my Australian shepherd, cocks her ears. She nudges me with each word she understands. "Look, grass!" (Nudge) "Ocean!" (Double nudge) "Birds!" (Sharp bark) "Happy." Lizzie jumps up and runs a few constricted crazy eights. Then she flops down and rolls on her back, grunting and moaning in pleasure. She rubs her muzzle in the grass, inhales its sweetness. Yes, happy.

The fog has lifted, revealing this to be the only flat surface in a vertical landscape. Mountains plummet to the sparkling ocean far below. White caps churn. Waves roll and break, but I cannot hear them. Vultures circle way lower than our grassy ledge.

Sweetie will have no part of this. She quivers in my lap, eyes beamed toward Nepenthe, worrying for her masters. She cannot bear for them to be out of sight. The dogs are a study in contrasts, the Agony and the Ecstasy. I massage Sweetie's neck and shoulders. I tell her everything is okay. Be in the moment, this beautiful moment. But she is always in the next moment, just like Mom and Dad. She explodes the myth that animals teach us to be in the present. Sweetie is panting herself into a frenzy, won't look at me when I call her name. The present moment is never enough. It's the next moment that counts—the next meal, the next adventure, the next acquisition.

Mom is making a second sweep through the gift shop. Dad is back in the café having a slab of apple pie that's almost the size of this patch of lawn. They are killing time because the tour of Post Ranch just up the road doesn't start until two in the afternoon.

"But what is there to do?" Mom always says when I take her to a place where there is "nothing but scenery." I had to lobby hard to persuade her to come. First she didn't want to leave the dogs at home. Then, when I found a hotel that welcomed them, she balked, "But we won't be able to leave them. They'll have to stay in the car."

"Don't worry. I'll take care of the dogs. It'll be beautiful."

"What will we do?"

"Just be there," I tell her, not comprehending the threat inherent in a scenic vacuum. Without distractions, Mom and Dad's fierce mental static takes over.

Over lunch the verbal grenades began to fly.

Dad: "That X is a goddamn horse's ass, isn't he?"

Mom: "Poor Y, what's she doing this weekend? Why isn't she dating that nice doctor?"

Dad (louder): "That X is a psalm-singing sonofabitch."

Mom: "Shut up, you're repeating."

Dad (loudest): "I said 'sonofabitch,' not 'horse's ass.' Stop nagging me. Your mother's a nudge. I'm gonna kill her."

Mom: (death rattling sigh)

Mom despairs that her grandchildren might never marry. She sees no promise of safety in their unsettled lives.

"They have no set, no dancing school, not even a Jewish group," she occasionally says to me. "Who will take care of them?"

She wants them to have exactly the same life she has had.

The seesaw of Mom and Dad's long marriage bounces from anger to despair, from joy to disappointment, before my eyes. The moments of calm are almost too fleeting to capture, but that balance point always includes dogs. For them our love is unconditional and constantly proclaimed. "Oh, what beauties!" sings Dad. "Look at the love in the dogs' eyes! The finest dogs in America!"

Dogs are the glue that bind us still, all except for Peter, who never shared this passion. Even as a little boy, my brother hung back, silently appraising us. We tell our family history through a succession of dogs as formalized as the British monarchy. Their posed portraits hang in Mom and Dad's dressing room: noble Punch, the mange-riddled spaniel of my childhood; Sam Basset, the riotous clown of my adolescence. During and after my college years I vaguely remember a string of unfortunate adoptees: George, a show basset, who hurled himself to a premature death off a cliff in Belvedere; Belle, a biting, unhousebroken dachshund who hid in a closet; and Mimi, a sweet but brainless corgi, who avoided umbrellas.

"Who is your favorite?" he always asks.

"Dad, I won't play that game. It creates unfavorites, and that makes me sad."

"Of course you have favorites. I certainly do."

He recites his list, then ranks the four grandchildren. Their status is precarious because none are producing great-grandchildren or even granddogs. Currently only our "royal princesses," Sweetie and Lizzie, bring joy. Under their reign, the seesaw of my parents' sixty-year marriage is stuck with Dad high on anger and Mom low in despair. I sit in the middle trying to shift my weight between them to achieve balance. But it's as if I have no weight at all. No matter what position I take, I cannot find the fulcrum. And now, petting Sweetie, trying to soothe her, I am equally ineffectual.

Why change? Sweetie gets what she wants: two unleashed walks a day with ample opportunity to chase bicycles, nip joggers, and eat garbage. Indoors, she has the run of the furniture and sleeps under the covers. Mom and Dad have gotten to eighty and beyond—teetering, tottering—without any help.

I think about this moment passing and want them to be lying here under this apple tree with me and the dogs in a dozy peace, sharing a stillness that's full, not yet knowing that Lizzie will soon be stung by a bee and worse, or that my Volvo's alternator belt is loose and the battery is going dead, or that the ache in Dad's legs is life threatening.

The Talking Dog

Moishe sees an ad in the paper for a talking dog for only ten dollars. He makes an appointment to meet the dog and his owner.

"So I hear you can talk?" says Moishe.

"Yes," says the dog. "I was born in Brooklyn and adopted by a family of immigrants. They spoke Yiddish and German, so the War Department sent me behind enemy lines to eavesdrop. I helped the Allies win. During the Cold War I learned Russian and spied on the Kremlin. I was the first dog in space, but that is still top secret. Now I work closer to home, helping rescuers locate trapped coal miners and missing children."

"Ai-yi-yi, I've never heard such a thing!" says Moishe. "Why are you selling him so cheap?"

"He's a liar. You can't believe a word he says."

The Brotherhood

Today I bring a peace offering, creamed herring, and arrive before lunch when the television is off. I don't want to compete with the TV judges who come on in the afternoon—Judge Wapner, Judge Joe Brown, and Judge Judy. Dad is hooked on Judge Judy and listens to her at full volume, but today I need his complete attention. Peter has let me in on a family secret, and I want to know more.

"Hi Dad. I brought you pickled herring."

"With sour cream?"

"Yes, your favorite."

"Oh, good."

"Dad, Peter tells me that John I. Walter fathered a secret child before he met Gaggy. He says the legal papers were found in Bobby's safe deposit box. Why there?"

"Jack Walter's legal papers were always kept in the Sinton family's safe."

"Why?"

"Because my uncle Edgar Sinton was Jack's brother-in-law. He'd married Marian Walter and was a lawyer and executor of Jack's will. After Edgar died, it all ended up in Bobby's safe deposit box. Look, if you're so interested, you can read the papers yourself. Come with me."

Dad scuttles to his office and pulls a worn manila envelope from a deep desk drawer.

"Here, take them. I don't need them. I can't read a thing."

San Francisco Aug. 10/1902.
1527 Green St.

Dear Jack:—

You will be surprised
to hear from me, but I want to
thank you for your settlement, and
I appreciate it greatly.
What prompted me to do what
I did, I will tell you.
I heard that you was going with
another girl, and that you had
got her in the same trouble that
I am in, at the same time,
I fully realized, that you would
not fulfill your promises,

82

Out tumble several thickly folded legal documents and three envelopes hand-addressed to D. N. & E. Walter Co. and marked "personal." I spread the evidence out around me on the floor in chronological piles, like shards from an archaeological dig.

The papers reveal that five years before John I. Walter had met and married Gaggy, he had fathered a son named John I. Walters [*sic*]. The child was born in January 1902 to a woman named Julia Linsley. Two months after his birth, a Superior Court document reveals that Julia Walters [*sic*], plaintiff, accused Jackson I. Walters [*sic*], defendant, of failing to provide "the necessaries of life." Three court documents dissolve "the bonds of matrimony," award custody to Julia, provide her with a $2,500 settlement, and release John I. Walter from all claims and demands "from the beginning of the world to Eternity."

What interests me far more than the numbing legalese of the court papers are three handwritten letters from Julia Linsley to my grandfather, John I. Walter. Who was the young woman behind the loopy, schoolgirl script with quill pen in hand and a broken heart? With each dip of the nib, the ink flows darkly for a word or two. Her sentences, liberally peppered with commas, are evenly spaced, determined, and legible. In her first letter she makes no mention of their seven-month-old son:

Dear Jack:

You will be surprised to hear from me, but I want to thank you for your settlement, and I appreciate it greatly. What prompted me to do what I did, I will tell you.

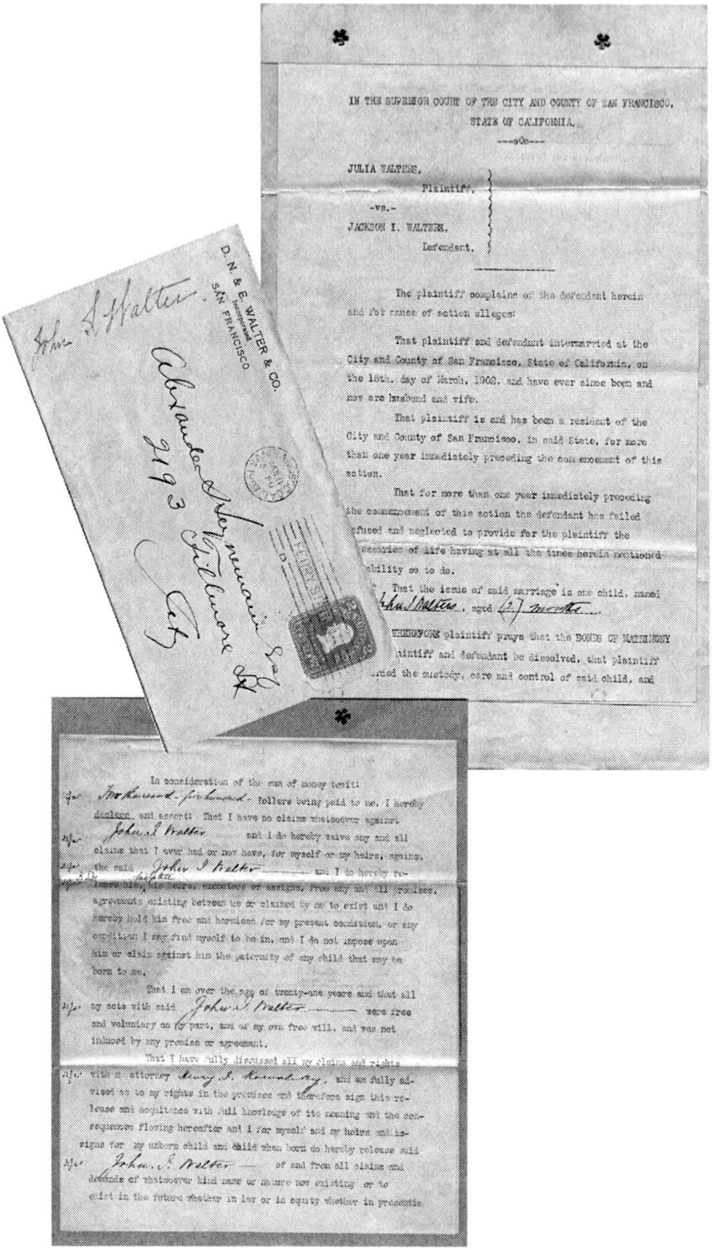

IN THE SUPERIOR COURT OF THE CITY AND COUNTY OF SAN FRANCISCO,
STATE OF CALIFORNIA.
---oOo---

JULIA WALTERS,
Plaintiff,
-vs.-
JACKSON I. WALTERS,
Defendant.

The plaintiff complains of the defendant herein and for cause of action alleges:

That plaintiff and defendant intermarried at the City and County of San Francisco, State of California, on the 18th. day of March, 1902, and have ever since been and now are husband and wife.

That plaintiff is and has been a resident of the City and County of San Francisco, in said State, for more than one year immediately preceding the commencement of this action.

That for more than one year immediately preceding the commencement of this action the defendant has failed [illegible]fused and neglected to provide for the plaintiff the [illegible]essaries of life having at all the times herein mentioned [illegible] ability so to do.

That the issue of said marriage is one child, named John I Walter, aged (2) months.

[illegible] THEREFORE plaintiff prays that the BONDS OF MATRIMONY [illegible] plaintiff and defendant be dissolved, that plaintiff [illegible] awarded the custody, care and control of said child, and

D. N. & E. WALTER & CO.
Incorporated
SAN FRANCISCO

John I. Walter

Alexander Hermann Esq
2193 Fillmore St
City

In consideration of the sum of money towit:
Two thousand - five hundred - Dollars being paid to me, I hereby declare and assert: That I have no claims whatsoever against John I. Walter and I do hereby waive any and all claims that I ever had or now have, for myself or my heirs, against the said John I Walter and I do hereby release him, his heirs, executors or assigns, from any and all promises, agreements existing between us or claimed by me to exist and I do hereby hold him free and harmless for my present condition, or any condition I may find myself to be in, and I do not impose upon him or claim against him the paternity of any child that may be born to me.

That I am over the age of twenty-one years and that all my acts with said John I. Walter were free and voluntary on my part, and of my own free will, and was not induced by any promise or agreement.

That I have fully discussed all my claims and rights with my attorney [illegible], and am fully advised as to my rights in the premises and therefore sign this release and acquitance with full knowledge of its meaning and the consequences flowing hereafter and I for myself and my heirs and assigns for my unborn child and child when born do hereby release said John I. Walter of and from all claims and demands of whatsoever kind name or nature now existing or to exist in the future whether in law or in equity whether in presentia

I heard that you was going with another girl, and that you had got her in the same trouble that I am in, at the same time. I fully realized, that you would not fulfill your promises, with me, a jealous woman will not stop, at anything.

I would not have blamed you one bit, for going with some one else, if I had refused to go out, when you wanted to, but I did not, in fact you did not go often enough.

I do not see how any one could have loved you, more than I did, I love you, and always will keep a place in my heart for you.

I signed the papers to release you for the future of all responsibility.

There is no future for me.

I will say good bye Jack please think of me kindly sometimes. J.L.

I reexamine the legal documents. I notice that Julia Linsley has initialed each paragraph in ink. Certainly a girl of her modest background could not have afforded her own lawyer. I imagine my grandfather, desperate to safeguard his fortune and reputation, engaging his lawyer friends. I imagine them standing over Julia, showing her where to initial and sign. Despite the signed declarations releasing John I. Walter from all claims, the secret saga continued.

Four years later a second note from Julia was hand-delivered to my grandfather. It was a rushed scrawl, scribbled on a scrap of torn paper:

December 17, 2006

I have been married since that time My name is Mrs. Neer and I have been divorced because he did not take care of me it has been 1 year last May, since I was granted a divorce. J.N.

The note had been folded and unfolded countless times. My grandfather carried it for a month in his vest pocket before forwarding it to his lawyer with a note of his own:

My dear Mr. Heynemann,

Enclosed the slip of paper, handed to Percy Kahn, by that party I spoke of at the telephone station near Van Ness and Turk on the 17th Dec. '06.

Yours, Jack Walter

The timing could not have been worse for my grandfather. He and his brother Gar had just become engaged to the beautiful Walter sisters, and the local society pages were about to trumpet the news of a double engagement. The marriages did take place without incident, and in 1908 Gaggy and John I. Walter had their first child, John Walter Jr.

The next surviving letter to my grandfather from Julia arrived in 1913. By then he and Gaggy had three children, John, Nell, and Marjorie:

San Francisco August 2, 1913

Dear Jack,

I am writing you in regard to little Jack. As you know heretofore my mother and sister and myself lived together, we were able to get along fairly well, my sister has lately got married as you know, and my mother has gone to Sausalito to live, leaving Jack and I alone. My monthly earnings are $49.50 out of which I have to support Jack and myself, you can readily see that this is insufficient, I do not want you to think I am about to ask you for any assistance for myself because, such is not my intention now, or at any other time, that was settled many years ago, but I do want you to help, with the boy's education and maintance, so he may be deciently clothed and feed, and thus given a fair chance in the world to earn his own living in a decent manner, As you must know little Jack is not physically developed to do hard manuel labor and therefore he will have to seek employment, in some walk of life, less arduous, he is now ten year's old, and in the fifth grade so the boy now is above the average. If you could see your way to letting me have for him twenty dollar's a month, until such time as he can go to work, it would pay for his food and clothes, the balance I am willing to pay myself.

I am particularly anxious for the child's sake, he shall not know anything concerning his birth, for I feel that should he do so, it might tinge his whole life, to his detriment. I would prefer, to not receiving the money directly from you, but through some third party whom you might name, so as not to compromise yourself. I have been very loath to write to you at all, and should not do so now, only I feel it is a duty I owe the boy.

I sincerely hope that you will receive this letter and consider it in the spirit in which it is written, and that you will let me know, your decission in the near future.

    Believe me,
    To remain
    Ever sincerely your's
    Mrs. J. Neer

I do not know if her plea was ever answered, for there is a seventeen-year gap in the record. Then, in 1930, Jack Neer surfaced upon the death of John I. Walter. Jack was twenty-seven years old, my grandfather's sole surviving son. Uncle Edgar arranged for a final payment of $10,070 on October 22, 1930, "in full satisfaction of any alleged or asserted claim."

I straighten the papers and see that Gaggy has written "John I. Walter" in her trademark purple ink across the front of an envelope addressed by him in 1907 to his attorney. I also find Gaggy's name on the final settlement drafted by Uncle Edgar in 1930.

I rush to show Dad.

"Dad, look! Gaggy knew! Here's proof!"

"Stop! Not another word!" says Dad. "Your grandmother was made of steel. If she knew, she never let on. It was verboten. When Gaggy wanted something gone, it was erased, just the way she banished Uncle Gar after Pearl died and he married his model, Betty. Gaggy never spoke of him again and wouldn't let him 'darken her doorstep.' Everyone had to sneak around behind her back. That's why your mother and her sisters went to Grindy's for tea on Wednesday afternoons. Grindy was Gar and John's mother, your mother's grandmother for God's sake!

A wonderful woman. That was the only way the girls could see their Uncle Gar. And when your mother and I got married in 1938, your mother had to slip out the back door so Uncle Gar could see her in her wedding dress. Gar was my uncle, too, you know."

"But, Dad, Mom and Marjorie must know about their half brother."

"No, they don't."

"I can't believe it. They should know. He probably has children and grandchildren. Somewhere they have nieces and nephews—"

"Don't be a shit disturber. What would be the point?"

"Secrets are demeaning. Mom would be fascinated—"

"How do you know? She idolized her father. I can't tell you the countless times she held him up to me as a paragon of manhood. Every time she criticized me she compared me to him. 'This is what a decent man would do.' How do you think that made me feel? And never once did I say a word. Not once. It made me sick, but I never told her."

Dad is up out of his armchair, lighting a cigarette and pacing.

"Look, if you think you know best, you tell her. But I'm not. It would bring back all her anger against me, and it would destroy her memory of him."

I am stunned. This man with no impulse control has kept a secret for more than sixty years! He is behaving rationally. His code of silence is self-serving because he belongs to the conspiracy of cheating men, but it's protecting Mom, too. I can't predict how she would react to these long-ago events. I only know the childlike happiness that floods her face whenever she tells me stories of her father:

> Every Sunday he took me out, just the two of us. One time we were riding in his new car. He had bought me an ice cream cone, and when he drove around a corner, the car swerved. The door on my side flew open. I fell out and cried because I'd lost my ice cream cone. He bought me another. I loved our outings.

Dad is right. Mom finds solace in these reveries of her father. She basks in being his last cherished child. I can't wreck her beautiful depiction. With a heavy heart I put the secret file back in its drawer and bow to the brotherhood of trusted men.

Max and the Mistress

Max and Moishe are longtime business partners and competitors. For years Moishe has had one gorgeous shiksa after another. Finally, one day Max gets lucky and meets this beautiful blonde, twenty-three-years-old, built like a gazelle. One thing leads to another, and pretty soon they are having an affair. Max decides to keep her and buys her an apartment not far from his office.

After thirty-eight years of marriage to Rachel, Max decides to tell her.

"Rachel, I'm telling you something wonderful: I'm having a mistress."

"A mistress? What is that?"

"You know, a mistress is something that fits between a mister and a mattress."

He shows her a picture of his shiksa.

"Oh, Max, I don't blame you. You're entitled. You're such a good man, a good father. Always so conscientious. You let Mama live with us. You remember my birthday. You deserve a little fun."

"Dear Rachel, you're such an understanding wife! I love you so much. Tell you what: I'll take you to Broadway. We'll see My Fair Lady, *then go to Lindy's for a snack."*

"Oh, Max, you're so generous! I'd love that."

Max gets tickets and takes her to the show several weeks later. Afterward they go to Lindy's for pastrami sandwiches with dill pickles. They are sitting at their table eating when Rachel looks up and says, "Max, isn't that Moishe Mendelbaum sitting at the booth in back?"

Max looks over his shoulder and says, "Yes, it is."

"But, Max, who's that woman he's with? It's not Bella."

"I know," says Max. "That's his mistress."

Rachel looks her over. "I like ours better."

Saturday Night Special

1997

At a hospital banquet honoring a revered, retiring internist, Ron and I are approached by Dr. B., a psychiatrist whom Dad consulted a few years ago—at Mom's insistence. He is an amiable man, now in his eighties, who loves Dad as a friend. After their formal sessions ended, they would lunch together. Dad charmed and amused him, just as he did so many others outside our family circle.

"How's your Dad?" Dr. B. asks warmly. His kind, Jewish face breaks into a crinkled smile. His jowls droop like melting candle wax.

"Not so good," I say. "His eyes have gotten much worse, and he's drinking and raging more than ever. At least he had the good sense to stop driving when he almost hit a dog."

"Ah yes, I love your father," says Dr. B., still smiling broadly.

For a moment I wonder if he has heard me, but I rush to reassure him, "Yes, he loves you, too. Your friendship really matters to him."

Dr. B. smiles back mistily, leans close, and says, "You know, he gave me his gun."

"Gun? Did you say 'gun'?"

"Yes, gun."

The hubbub around us stops. Gun?

Dad is the most vehemently anti-gun person I know. How many times he's lectured us at the dinner table about the stupidity of gun ownership: "You've got to be a damned fool to keep a gun in the house. They cause accidents, don't prevent them. And anyone could use it against you. Crazy to keep a gun."

"Do you mean a hunting shotgun?" I ask Dr. B., remembering Poppa's shotgun that Dad kept at the duck club.

"No," says Dr. B. "It was a small handgun, a Saturday Night Special." He smiles proudly, as if Dad had paid him the profoundest compliment.

The party closes in, parting us. We are seated at different tables. I have never seen a handgun up close, but I feel as if Dr. B. has just shoved one in my face. I try to imagine what desperation could have motivated Dad. He knew too well what a handgun can do. Over twenty years ago Bobby's first son, Michael, exactly my age, had committed suicide with a shotgun. Dad had been the one to go to the coroner's to identify the body. He told me afterward that he could bear to look only at Michael's shoes, nothing else. Michael wore size 12.

A chilling fear takes hold of me—I'm certain that Dad must have meant to kill himself. What if he's got another gun?

As soon as I can, I rush to a telephone to call Peter. I repeat every word of my encounter with Dr. B.

"Oh my God," says Peter. "Dad could have another gun. Do you think he'll use it against Mom or me?"

"No, no, Peter, he'd never do that. Never," I insist, stunned by Peter's reaction.

"Jesus, maybe none of us is safe!"

"Oh, Peter, he'd use it against himself first."

"How can you be so sure? With all his drinking and raging? He's out of control. He's been kicked out of every bar in town. I know he'd shoot me first."

The depth of Peter's fear shocks me. I can imagine Dad capable of suicide but never murder. My experience of Dad does not prepare me for this. As Dad's declared favorite I've known his tender side. I remember his gentleness when I was seven and had fallen while running across the rickety wooden bridge at Rampart. My arms bristled with splinters from elbow to wrist. Dad set to removing each one himself with a sterilized needle and tweezers.

I grew up knowing Dad was my ally. Peter knew him as a bully. When we were adults, Peter became a super sleuth, sniffing out Dad's whereabouts and dealings, while I tended to the home front, keeping the peace and fending off the hurts. I sensed Dad's vulnerability in his excessive need for attention and in his persistent suffering over bygone slights. I often lament that I was born Dad's daughter and not the attentive mother he should have had.

Peter and I argue our different viewpoints back and forth.

"He hates himself, not you," I say.

Peter threatens to rush over and search the house immediately, but I dissuade him until I've talked to Dr. B.

"How can you trust him?" asks Peter. "He's already violated doctor-patient confidentiality."

"You're right, but it's the best we can do right now. Wait 'til I call you back."

Later I telephone Dr. B. from home to ask if he thinks Dad could be a danger to himself or to anyone else.

"Your Dad? Nahhh. Never."

Peter is not convinced, nor am I. Neither of us knows for certain whether there is a gun in the house. Until now I thought we were just playing games.

Rabinowitz at the Costume Ball

The B'nai B'rith Lodge 132 is having its annual costume party. Rabinowitz goes to Katz's costume shop and says, "I want to win first prize, guaranteed."

Katz brings out a Louis XIV costume with a wig of ringlets, a pink silk shirt with ruffles down the front, a lace handkerchief, satin pants with cummerbund, and high-heeled shoes with silver buckles and pointed toes.

"Louis XIV: guaranteed first prize."

"How much is costing such a costume?"

"Fifty dollars."

"You got something cheaper maybe?"

Katz goes to the back room and returns with a Lord Nelson costume with a black ostrich feather in the helmet, a double-breasted red jacket with brass buttons, black jodhpurs, and knee-high riding boots.

"Lord Nelson: maybe guaranteed second prize."

"How much is costing such a costume?"

"Twenty-five dollars."

"You got something cheaper maybe?"

Katz brings out a Captain Hook costume with a red bandana, a black eye patch, a white blouse, a leather vest, dungarees, and a metal hook for a hand.

"Captain Hook: maybe guaranteed third prize."

"How much is costing such a costume?"

"Fifteen dollars."

"You got something cheaper maybe?"

"Look," says Katz, "for two dollars: Next door is a paint shop. Buy one quart of red paint. Go to bakery shop and buy some spangles. Then, go to hardware store and buy a broomstick unless you have one. You go home to shower. Then pour the paint all over you, sprinkle on the spangles, and put the broomstick up your ass. You're a candied apple on a stick!"

Crossword Puzzle

September 9, 1997

This afternoon Mom has had cataract surgery. I've come back to the hospital to bring her home. She is sitting up, in her crumpled cotton CP Shades travel outfit, atop a hospital bed, working the crossword puzzle, oblivious to Tom Brokaw, her favorite anchor, who delivers the evening news from the TV monitor above the bed.

She is all dressed except for her shoes, size-4 Ferragamos, paired neatly beside the bed. Peter and I used to tease her about her tiny feet, "bound feet" we called them. The truth behind that joke saddens me now—the secrets, the solidarity of men, the weight of convention that keep her bound.

While Mom works the puzzle, my eyes are on her, trying to crack the genetic code. I am the only woman in my family who doesn't do the daily crossword. Mom does them religiously, just as Gaggy did. My daughter, Kate, does them, too, but I've never been tempted. The clues leave me cold. I don't like games that have rigid grids and right answers. Correct answers are not necessarily truthful.

Am I the weak link in a chain of three strong-willed women who try to impose consistency on a blighted, chaotic world? I am guessing. There is no answer sheet for the questions that puzzle me. Why do people do these things—choose the blinders of daily ritual that obscure what's really happening?

All three are women of their word. They keep promises. They remember birthdays and anniversaries. They make lists of daily tasks that get done. They return phone calls and send thank-you notes promptly. They pay bills ahead of time and balance their checkbooks. They make restaurant reservations. They are never late or idle. They do not wallow in emotional quagmires.

Gaggy, a renowned bookbinder and rare books collector, devoted her life to the printed word. She made signs with gold tooling. The one that sits behind glass in a gold frame on Mom's dresser says, "DO IT NOW."

But Mom never does the crossword puzzle first thing. Instead, she takes it with her through her tightly scheduled days. Like her mother, she is a nationally recognized craftsman. She serves on the board of trustees for the American Craft Council. Only late in the day will she permit herself to savor the crossword. "I like to look forward to it," she says, like a dog coddling a juicy bone.

Mom always does the crossword in blue ballpoint, which shows the strength of her commitment, I think. Her capital letters carve greasy grooves in the squares. Extravagant doodles fill the margins, full of voluptuous curves and bold patterns.

Every football Sunday of my high school years, while Mom solved the crossword puzzle, I got to join the brotherhood of men at the 49ers game. I walked with Dad, Peter, Uncle Stanley, Stephen, and various male cousins to Kezar Stadium in Golden Gate Park. My oldest cousin, Margot, and I were the only female regulars, which made me feel specially chosen. Occasionally a breathy blonde with a false English accent would accompany Stanley, but never regularly.

We sat in the top row at the fifty-yard line, the best view of the field, Dad insisted. I knew the name, height, and weight of every player on the team, hated their wives, and harbored secret crushes on four: fast Hugh McElhenny (#39), solid Joe Perry (#34), towering Leo "The Lion" Nomellini (#73), and blue-eyed Matt Hazeltine (#55).

The tweedy bulk of men pressed in on every side. I loved the bawdy ribaldry of the season-ticket holders—their raucous voices, their cigarette smoke and sloshing beer. I huddled between Dad and Stanley or Stephen, safe in the proximity of my big, ingrown family. On rainy days our umbrellas would tangle, trapping body heat and furtive hugs, while the splashing runoff poured onto the broad backs of the regulars who sat in front of us. A flask would travel down the row, and I would pass it on. We would become emboldened and shout out our winning plays. Interception! Alley-Oop to R.C. Owens! Hand-off to McElhenny! And then, as if we'd willed it, The Blitz! In a sudden chorus of unleashed passion, we'd jump up in unison, cheering or jeering until we were hoarse.

Mom's eyeglasses are wedged on over the bulky bandage.

"How was it?" I ask.

"Fine," she says, scrutinizing the puzzle with her good eye. Her pen pauses.

"Could you feel anything?"

"Nothing. It was nothing. Hmmm, seven letters, 'swallow one's pride' . . ."

"Should you be using your eye like that?"

"What are you talking about?"

"I needed to rest mine after my cataract surgery," I tell her. She pays no attention. The puzzle has her in its thrall.

"Why do you do crosswords?"

"It's like meditation," Mom says. "It blots out everything else." Like the blaring television turned up full volume in the living room, where Dad boozes and stokes the rage that fuels his nightly dinner blather? Or her shame for putting up with this? These outbursts are not part of her game plan. They violate the unspoken rules. Am I a bad sport for noticing or a weakling to keep playing along? There is too much at stake.

While the women do crossword puzzles and pencil social events in the calendar slots, the men play and plot. The contents of Bobby's safe deposit box were to be kept from the blood-related women. Mom and her sisters have no knowledge of their half brother, who in turn had a son and grandchildren. Somewhere I have more cousins. Only the men, the macho brotherhood of cheating men, are privy to this information.

Down girl! they said when I got too exuberant. *Don't rock the boat!* came the warning when I challenged their pronouncements. *Who do you think you are?* was the cry when my pride or ambition got too bold. And when my probing of the past became too personal, *Let sleeping dogs lie.*

The game is rigged! I want to shout. *Dad cheats. He hides the answer sheet. He has never told you about your father's . . .*

peccadillo? affair? liaison? These words diminish the event. They erase Julia Linsley and "little Jack." How disagreeable of me to object. After all, men do what they do on the sly in order to protect the women who are their wives. Isn't that highly moral?

"'Henry VIII apologist, Bishop Hugh—'?" Mom asks, hard at work on the puzzle.

"You know I can't do those things," I say.

Above the hospital bed Paula Jones pouts from the TV monitor. She refuses to settle her case against President Clinton and has fired her lawyers.

"Wait, I've got the third and fifth letters. It'll come out."

"How many times have you been in a hospital?" I ask.

Mom's ballpoint writes, stops, then taps the paper as she counts.

"Once for an ovarian cyst. Twice for childbirth. Twice for miscarriages. Once when I was born, but that doesn't count. I was the only one born in a hospital."

The ballpoint continues.

"That counts. You mean Gaggy's first three were born at home?"

Mom at eighty is the youngest. The banished child, her half-brother, would be over ninety, if he is still alive. What a hefty penance John I. Walter paid when his legitimate namesake was the one to die.

"Uh huh . . . 'a large marsh near Virginia Beach'? Hmm . . ." The pen goes to the next row.

"Do you remember giving birth?"

"No. They knocked us out in those days. With ether." Mom looks up from the puzzle. "I can't remember anything. No one ever talked about it."

"Not even your sisters?"

"No."

Her eye returns to the grid again. The pen writes and stops. "Sultans of swing, top 40 group?" The pen hovers.

"Really? If you didn't discuss childbirth, what did you talk about? Your husbands?"

"Sometimes. 'Mild expletive' . . . D-A-R-N. Ha, they always use that. 'Proofreader's word' . . . D-E-L-E-T-E. That's easy. There're lots of stock phrases."

"Were any of them faithful?"

"Mmmm . . ." The pen is writing again. It stops, taps, and quickly goes on to the next column. "Ha. 'His wife was the pillar of the community,' three letters. Easy. 'Weasel cousin'? That'll come out. It always comes out."

The secret hovers between us as palpably as the flickering rays of the TV monitor. I want her to know, but the secret is not mine to tell. D-E-L-E-T-E it, I tell myself. Her life is hard enough. Her pen is writing quickly now. On some level, I think, she must know. The puzzle is almost done. She will not give up.

"'*It's Always Something* author' . . . six letters ending with R," Mom smiles nostalgically.

"Oh, I know that one!" I cry out. "Radner, Gilda Radner. I miss her, too. Do you ever cheat and use the answer sheet?"

"No, no. I usually figure them out on my own."

I gather up the rest of the newspapers and fold them into her satchel along with her post-op instructions. Then I reach out to help her down from the high bed.

"Stop treating me like an old person," she says swinging her feet over the edge. "I don't need you to be so solicitous."

Carnival Life

For years Lennie Kleinberg has worked at the local carnival cleaning up after the dancing elephants' act. One night he comes home to his wife, Bubbie, in a terrible mood.

"Oy vey, all day long I shovel shit. Look, Bubbie, my clothes are filthy. My shoes are a mess. I can't get the grime out from under my nails or the stink out of my nose."

"Poor shlemiel," says Bubbie. "Why don't you quit?"

"What—and give up show business?"

Poppa's Favorites

Sam has been a widower for twenty years and suffers from arthritis, but recently his luck has changed, and he's married a beautiful younger woman eager for sex.

During a routine visit to his arthritis doctor, Sam tells him he's been married about a month but is "having trouble getting it in."

The doctor asks, "Have you tried Vaseline?"

"That makes it hard?"

Fat lady Mendelbaum tips the scale at three hundred pounds. One day she goes to her doctor.

"Hello, Mrs. Mendelbaum," says the doctor. "You don't look so well today. Is anything the matter?"

"Oh, doctor, I'm so sad. Very upset. My Moishe, I love him so much, but I don't seem to appeal to him anymore . . ."

She takes out a hanky and starts to cry.

"Well, Mrs. Mendelbaum, could you diet?"

"Yes, but what color?"

Q. How do you stop a Jewish girl from having sex?

A. Marry her.

Eenie, Meenie, Miney, Mo

May 30, 1998

Nelia, Dad's new helper, has had another sleepless night.

"Mr. Henry has gotten better at controlling his temper in front of me, but now he's getting fresh," Nelia tells Peter and me. "He says I'm so short and fat that I should sue the city for building the sidewalks too close to my butt. And last night while I was at the stove, he tried to pinch my bottom!

"I can no longer go along with his bad jokes. Now he's saying, 'Let's kill Miss Carol and run away together.' He wants me and my friend Cora to drive him on an overnight trip through the Feather River Canyon so he can see it before he goes blind. This is not my job. I will not come back to work until you have had a family meeting to get things under control."

We quickly agree. Peter arranges with Mom to expect us for lunch for a family "bow-wow" but not to tell Dad. From past confrontations, we fear it will be ugly. The point we need to drive home today is that Mom needs Nelia even if he doesn't.

Peter and I arrive promptly at noon and confer on the doorstep. I admire Peter, the unfavored, for showing up at all. In Dad's distorted view, Peter hovers like a greedy vulture, appraising the spoils that will one day be his.

"I'll start by listing Nelia's complaints," says Peter. "Then you, the appeaser, can take over."

"Okay."

"We have to have clear ground rules. From this moment on, nothing will be the same!"

We shake hands nervously and enter the house.

Dad, slumped in his living room armchair, is in a fierce snit today. Says his legs hurt more than ever, and he wants to be left alone. No, it's too early for lunch; he doesn't want any. Eat without him.

"But Dad," Peter says kindly, "I've taken off from the *Chronicle* and have only an hour. Just come to the dining room and sit with us if you don't want to eat."

Reluctantly and uncharacteristically, Dad agrees. We seat ourselves in a slightly altered arrangement of our age-old pattern: Dad at the head of the table, Mom to his right, and Peter to Mom's right in my accustomed place. I am in Peter's former hot seat beside Dad. My throat closes up completely; I can't swallow. Peter, who usually inhales his food, doesn't touch his lunch either.

Peter says, "Dad, we have to have a family meeting because Nelia has threatened to quit."

Dad throws his napkin to the floor, slams both hands down on the table, and bolts from his chair.

"Goddamnit, so help me God. Don't say that name. That BITCH!" and he is off, racing to the living room.

I am out of my chair in a flash, blocking his way, screaming, "Shut up! Shut up!" My voice cracks as he keeps going. I grab his shoulders and shove him back. We struggle and swat at each other until I get a sharp grip on his bony upper arms. Despite his shrinkage, he's incredibly strong and wiry. It takes all my strength to push him back to his place and force him into his chair.

"We have ALL got to be here," I screech, jamming his shoulders down each time he tries to rise. His mouth is open. His eyes are frantic. If this were water, I'd be drowning him, holding him under until he turns limp. For the first time I understand crimes of passion.

When Dad stops resisting, I let go and settle into my own chair, disgusted with myself. I have just assaulted my own father. This is elder abuse. Sweetie shakes and pants under the table. Across from me Mom silently eats her lunch. I spread my napkin across my lap and straighten the fork. In a high, tight, school-marmish voice, I hear myself saying, "We will all get a chance to talk. It will be your turn, too, but first you have got to listen."

While my pulse races, Peter gazes at me with amazement. For once I have stuck my scrawny neck out. He tells me later that Dad and I looked like two roosters going for the kill in a cockfight. Peter's face melts into a smile as he takes over, sounding like a seasoned mediator.

In a calm, measured voice, he says, "Dad, we want to hear your side of the story, too, but most of all we must come up with a solution that will work for everyone. We all have to deal with limits. Things you may have done or said in the past are considered harassment these days. Nelia's perception is that you have crossed a line."

"Fuck her perception," Dad yells. He is up and out of his chair, bolting this time out onto the deck beyond the dining room. "I hate this p.c. crap," he bellows to the sky. "The fool can't take a joke. Her problems! What about MY problems?"

Peter and I race onto the deck, too, shouting back incongruous affirmations, incongruous because the sharpness in our voices doesn't match the sympathy we'd like our words to convey. We yell for all the neighborhood to hear how hellish it must be to be going blind and deaf.

"Goddamn right!" shouts Dad.

"How terrible to have your legs giving out."

"Tell me about it," he says, his voice breaking.

"How terrifying to grow old and to lose all the people you grew up with."

Tears are coursing down our faces.

"But, Dad, other people have done it," says Peter.

"There are other ways than rage," I say. "We want to help."

Peter guides Dad back inside to his dining chair.

"Dad, you're like a furnace," he says. "You're too hot to touch. We don't want to get close. We'll get singed."

"You've perfected anger," I say. "It's your daily practice, like calisthenics, and you're a pro. You've elevated it to a high art."

Dad looks directly at us and smiles. Right! For once he's understood, and he's back where he wants to be, the center of attention on his terms.

"But Dad, we can't take it. We don't have your stamina," I add, "or Mom's. It's as if I've developed an allergy to your rages. I've lost my tolerance. And Mom, you can't expect other people to endure what you endure. It's too much. It's way beyond normal."

"Look, Dad," Peter says. "We're all you have left. I'm sorry it's that way, but it is. And we aren't abandoning you."

"I think I'd like that," quips Dad.

"Back to Nelia," says Peter.

"BULLSHIT!" screams Dad, and he is off on a rant. "Look, this is my house, and I'm boss. If Nelia can't cope, she can find another job. You're all a bunch of fools to believe what she says. You're so quick to take her word over mine. And Peter, you always take the side of my opponent."

The charge is so patently false that I fly up out of my chair and stand over him with my face to his, beady eyeball to beady eyeball. In a voice so dripping with sarcasm that it pierces my soul, I hiss, "Well, aren't you a treasure? Aren't you a gem of humanity? Just the kind of person we want for a father."

Dad stares back at me, mouth agape. He pales and shrinks from me. He has heard my acid words, every one, and he is as shocked as I am. I have never used such a cruel tone against him—or anyone—and his swift compliance makes me realize it is a weapon he knows too well. It is the staple of his upbringing that kept him in check, bullied and beaten. The hurt smolders still and ignites all other rages. I am cruel to have sunk this low to get his attention. It is no victory. I return to my chair feeling sick at heart.

Peter manages to pick up the thread. He recites the ground rules. If Dad is belligerent and out of control in his presence, he will ask Dad to calm down. If he can't and we are in a restaurant, Peter will drive him home or send him in a taxi. If we are at one of our houses, we'll ask Dad to go to another room. Peter's policy is "zero tolerance," and he asks Mom and me to back him up. We agree too quickly. I know Mom will never follow through, though in that fleeting moment I think I will.

Mom chimes in with the name of a geriatric psychiatrist who might help Dad deal with anger. Dad grudgingly agrees to see the guy—for our sakes, not his. None of us mentions drinking because we have lost that round too many times before.

Peter has to get back to work and leaves feeling euphoric. I see him to the front door, and he says, "We did it! We laid down the rules. I feel exonerated."

He tells me I was magnificent, but I am devastated. I can't leave without offering something nice and upbeat. I go back upstairs to tell Dad I will drive him through the Feather River Canyon since Nelia can't. He accepts the offer and gives me the maps he has collected from the auto association. The itinerary is all mapped out.

Then I remember that Peter, Bev, Ron, and I have made plans to take Mom and Dad and the dogs to the Carmel Valley for their sixtieth wedding anniversary in less than ten days.

"Do you still want to go to Carmel Valley?" I ask.

"Sure," says Dad.

"Why not?" says Mom.

And I drive home to Berkeley in a daze, wondering if any of this ever really happened.

By evening I have proof: 80 proof Smirnoff. A very soused Dad phones, enraged at me for being disloyal. We should not have listened to Nelia at all. The right thing to do would have been to tell her to talk to him directly. He repeats himself three times, not wanting a response, and slams down the receiver.

Hopeless, hopeless. I vow to retreat from mortal combat. I will go to the Carmel Valley and, later in the summer, to the Feather River. I will be polite. I will avoid confrontation. I will hide in the wings and wait for an opportunity. There has to be a better way. Nice might not have the power to change him, but neither does nasty.

Fat Lady Epstein

You remember the fancy condo on Riverside Drive? Well, the same Mrs. Epstein who lives on the sixth floor and her husband, Heimie, are having a terrible time sweating out a heat wave: 92 degrees all week with 95 percent humidity. It is Sunday morning, and already it is hot. Mrs. Epstein gets up, takes off her nightgown. She is fat. Her flesh sags like water balloons. She is sweating like a pig. She goes into the bathroom to pishen.

Heimie has just finished in the bathroom and has left the toilet seat up. But fat Mrs. Epstein sits down without looking and falls in.

"Heimie! Heimie!" she calls. "Help me! I'm stuck. Get me out!"

Heimie comes running and tries with all his might, but she is slippery with sweat, and he can't budge her.

"You're stuck tight as a cork in a champagne bottle!"

"Call the fire department," wails Mrs. Epstein. "and cover me with something."

Heimie gets 911, then rushes back to the bathroom, yanks down the shower curtain, and wraps it around her.

"No, no," she cries. "I'm still naked. The firemen will see my fuzzies."

"Here," says Heimie, "take my yarmulke and cover your pubies."

The firemen arrive, and Heimie waits in the living room while they struggle to free her. He hears all kinds of heaving and grunting and thumping around. Then, finally, a huge splash.

A very wet fireman emerges from the bathroom and says, "Your wife's gonna be all right, but the rabbi's a goner."

Medical Marvel

December 8, 1998

Dad does not suffer silently. He thrashes and swears. The pains in his legs have become so crippling that this Thanksgiving, for the first time, he was unable to cook the turkey. He can hardly stand. His feet are frigid and blue. When he crumples over in a cold sweat with dizziness, Mom says, "Oh, he always does that."

Ron listens with his stethoscope and cannot find a pulse in either leg. He knows better than to speculate about the possibility of amputation to Mom, who rejects alarmist doctors and walks away from news she does not want to hear. So far, denial has served her well, but I know Dad is scared.

Later I drop by their house, in case Dad wants to talk. I find him deep in vodka-sharpened thought, on a positive track constructing logic problems that have concrete answers. He reviews from memory old algebra equations, brainteasers, and geometric theorems with solid proofs.

He shushes me because he's calculating the date on which he will equal the age that Bobby lived to be, forty-six days short of his eighty-second birthday. Dad is sixty-two days away from turning eighty-two. He turns his failing eyes to the ceiling and counts on his fingers. In sixteen days, on December 17, he will be the same age Bobby was when he died—eighty-one years, ten months, and thirteen days.

I'm quite sure Dad wants to live as long as Bobby did. Sibling rivalry goads him still, but I don't know if he wants to live much beyond that. I file away December 17 warily, and my mind goes blank. I cannot imagine what I will feel when he dies. Sadness? Shock? Invigoration? Relief? I hope I will feel something. This constant numbness is worse than grief.

Ron finds a vascular surgeon who locates blockages in Dad's femoral arteries. At daybreak on December 8 Dad is scheduled for angiograms to map out the tangle of calcified congestion. Later that same day the surgeon will insert Teflon tubing to bypass the clogged sections.

Two days before the surgery Dad phones in wild agitation. He has 160,000 frequent flyer miles that might expire before he does, and he wants them cashed in before the operation. Where should we go?

"Who?" I stammer.

"You, Mom, and me. Who else? Fool."

Another trip, so soon? I tell him I'll research it and get back to him.

"Just do it. Now. And be sure to use up all the miles. I don't care where."

"What about Hawaii?" I ask, even though I know he hates Hawaii or anyplace with sun and sand.

"You and your mother decide. Just settle it before I go to the hospital."

From San Francisco, Hawaii is an easy nonstop flight that consumes the most free miles. Since Ron already has plans to be in Maui the first week of June with his windsurfing buddies, I decide to lobby Mom for a plush resort on the leeward side of the island. Mom loves travel, even to Hawaii with her memories of its rain-soaked boredom and terrible food. Mom agrees to Maui because a Four Seasons has opened in Wailea. Too frugal to stay there, she settles for a seven-day package deal that provides car and condo close enough to enjoy the Four Seasons' grounds and amenities. With visions of soufflés and foie gras dancing in her head, Mom declares we'll eat dinners in their fancy dining rooms. The lure of Hawaii six months from now gets our minds off Dad's impending operation. Even if we never get there, it's already having a salutary effect.

On surgery day, December 8, I bring Mom to the hospital after Dad's early-morning angiogram. We plan to wait with him until the big surgery scheduled for two PM. Dad is an impaled hornet, tied on his back to a gurney, with restraints to keep the insertion wounds in his arteries from hemorrhaging. I angle around an IV drip to inspect his face, which is surprisingly unwrinkled and pink when he is lying down. I tell him the radiologist said the angiogram went perfectly.

"Fucking shit!" he roars. "Tell him to go fuck himself. Doctors are so goddamned pleased with themselves. Assholes."

Dad's expletives echo down the hospital corridors. Obscenities ricochet off the walls. Everything is wrong.

"This is torture. I can't lie this still. I need a cigarette. Being on my back for hours is excruciating. I'm hungry, thirsty, miserable. No one comes to help. This is worse than hell. Goddamnit."

Spent nurses glance at us from the nursing station. They know the score: another alcoholic smoker going into withdrawal. The usual sedatives and painkillers will backfire, agitating him more. An orderly approaches, bearing ice chips.

"Fuck you, fat Skibby."

"Henry, stop that," Mom whispers. "If you keep this up, we're leaving."

He does, and we bolt. We run through the maze of long, squeaky linoleum hallways to the elevator. We press the down button and don't look back. We ride all the way to the lobby without speaking. For once Mom's reacting the way I've been wanting her to.

Out on the sidewalk in the bright sunlight I feel giddy with release. Someone else is taking care of him! We are free!

"Let's have a party," I say. "Let's invite Peter and Bev and Ron for dinner. I'll make it."

"No," she says. "Alex is there tonight. He should cook."

I ask her what Alex likes to make.

"He does a good steak, but we had that last night. Ugh, I'm so tired of everything. I don't want to think about it now. I'll go to the market this afternoon."

"No, let me."

"No, no," she insists. "I can do it."

And we are locked in our familiar stranglehold, me offering help, she resisting. We go back and forth, but she refuses, "Absolutely not."

Mom shops for food daily because she can't decide what she wants to eat until that day arrives. She likes an uncluttered pantry. Peter and I know the paltry contents of the shelves by heart: two or three tins of sardines, one jar of applesauce, bottled clam juice, a four-ounce can of tomato juice, several cans of dog food. Peter is certain that some of the label designs date from the early '50s.

On a bountiful day there will be a new can of Boston baked beans or Del Monte apricots, and maybe a tin of deviled ham, but never beer or Calistoga or fillers like chips and cereal.

When Mom and I get back to the house, I inspect the refrigerator and find mostly empty shelves. The naked interior feels indecent. Certainly there had been food here when Peter and I were growing up. When had famine set in?

In a lettuce drawer I find poorly wrapped leftovers: a graying wedge of last night's avocado and a bite of yesterday's grilled cheese sandwich intended for tomorrow's lunch. I throw out the slimy remains of a head of butter lettuce, a wizened carrot grown hairy, and some liquified scallions. I know better than to toss the prized half-eaten artichoke heart or the sliver of berry pie or the leathery chicken drumstick. How can I trust anything that comes out of these sorry drawers?

"I'm ravenous," I say to Mom. "Let's ask Alex to cook something ethnic."

"Yuk, Philippine food."

"He makes good chicken curry. Let's have curry. It goes a long way."

By evening Dad is wheeled to the ICU after four hours of surgery. I apologize to his pleasant, smiling surgeon that Dad is such a difficult patient.

"Look," Dr. G. says, "he's nearly eighty-two and full of life. You've got to respect that."

His words help me relax. Dad is safe.

Dinner without Dad turns out to be a gift. It's as if we have won a deluxe vacation with expenses paid by Medicare. Mom bathes before dinner and changes into silk hostess slacks and a kimono. Peter serves her a glass of wine. Beverly has made hors d'oeuvres.

Alex's curry is delicious and plentiful. Mom says she has never seen so much food in her life. We have seconds and thirds. Alex has made a layer cake for dessert: four-stories high with rococo icing. He used to be a baker. I'm glad Dad isn't here to criticize his effort. He would insist that such a cake with its buttercream frosting tastes too store-bought, and he would repeat his condemnation loudly and mercilessly to override our disagreement whether voiced or not.

It is so unnatural to be at the dinner table without Dad that for most of the meal we talk about him. Ron, who was the last to look in on Dad, translates what the doctors have told him. After a night in the ICU Dad will be moved to a two-person room on the medical floor for at least four days. He predicts that Dad will be able to resume his normal activities in three to four weeks. Mom brightens at the news—not that Dad is doing well after surgery, for she never doubted that, but that he will be staying in the hospital, then taking it easy while he recuperates.

We return to the living room to chat about other topics. Mom falls sound asleep sitting up in her armchair. She is exhausted. More than any of us, she needs this hospitalization.

On December 10, day 2 post-op, Bev and I visit Dad in his room on Four South. We bring his favorite throat lozenges and chocolates. The door to his room is closed. After knocking several times we enter timidly and find his bed empty. His roommate is snoring heavily in an oxygen tent. A shuffling noise in the closet catches our attention. We peer in, and there is Dad in his hospital johnny rifling through the belongings in his satchel. An unlit cigarette hangs from his lips, and his trembling hands remove a lighter from his jacket pocket. As he turns around and emerges, a nurse barges in and catches him red-handed.

"My God! There's oxygen in use here. You can't smoke."

She grabs the lighter and hustles Dad back to bed.

"He was up all night, poking around the room with his cane. He flooded the bathroom."

"How?" Bev and I ask in unison.

"He left the faucet on full blast," she says and secures the door in its most open position. She glares at Dad before she leaves. "See that it stays like this."

"Jesus, Dad, I thought you'd be out of it. Can I see your scar?"

He arranges the sheets over his privates and lifts the johnny. A great ropey scar bisects his groin. Two more lead down his thighs. The knotty wounds appear to be stapled shut and glued.

"You're some trussed bird," I say.

"That's no way to talk to your father."

At quarter of eight the next morning, December 11, Dad phones Mom.

"Come get me. I'm coming home."

"But Henry," she says. "I'm still in bed. I'll eat breakfast and get dressed and come for you at nine."

"No, I won't wait. I'll take a taxi."

By eight thirty in the morning Dad is home, escaped

from the hospital AWOL and in the kitchen cooking bacon and eggs. Four strips of bacon make up for the ones he'd missed during his hospital stay.

Within four days of his surgery, Dad is car shopping. Mom phones on the evening of December 12 to report that he hasn't come home yet.

"From where?" I ask.

"The Lexus dealer in Daly City."

To surprise Mom, Dad had negotiated to buy her a used Lexus before his operation. He needed Alex to drive them to the dealer so that Mom could help him with the paperwork, which he can't read. After an hour Mom had gotten bored and left with Alex. The salesman promised to arrange for someone to drive Dad home later in the new car.

"But that was four hours ago," says Mom. "It's dark now, and the dealership has closed."

I tell her to wait another half hour. "They probably had to wait 'til closing time to find a driver plus another car and driver who could caravan clear across town."

My hunch proves correct.

To my amazement, the Lexus turns out to be flawless—not a nick, not a scratch, with low mileage and two years left on the warranty. Dad paid halfway between wholesale and retail bluebook value, not a penny more.

The next morning, Dad has Alex drive him in the new Lexus to an unused airfield down in the Presidio. He and Alex switch places, and Dad drives Alex round and round, forward and backward, in blind circles. The car checks out perfectly, and Dad phones to tell me he's still a marvelous driver.

Grim Diagnosis

Three anthropologists, an Englishman, a Frenchman, and a Jew, are working in Africa when they come down with a rare tropical disease. The doctor tells them they have but six months to live.

"I shall go to my favorite trout stream in Scotland," says the Englishman, "and I will take along my pipe and all the books I have intended to read."

The Frenchman says, "I will go to St. Tropez on the French Riviera, drink the finest wine, and make love every night to a different woman."

The Jew says, "I will get another doctor."

Blind Man's Bluff

April 23, 1999

Peter and I start disowning Dad semantically. After especially bruising episodes we sometimes refer to him in the third person: "Your father phoned four times in a half hour tonight and hung up on me twice."

"I got a call from the broker. Your father has started risky option trading from Mom's account."

This trick of grammar objectifies Dad and helps us catch our breath before we reenter the fray . . .

Say yes when your mostly blind-deaf father wants to bring his yap dog and live with you while your mother is visiting dear friends in Washington, D.C. Do not be surprised when he arrives toting a bag of squabs and a package of wild rice but no clothing. He doesn't like to change clothes anymore, but he lives to cook. Let him roam around the kitchen feeling for the sharpest knives, and don't offer him an apron or he'll shout, "I NEVER wear an apron!" If you hover, he'll say, "Get out of my way." And don't remind him to smoke outdoors because he already knows that rule and rules exist to be broken. Like promises. Keep pretending you don't know he's been drinking vodka.

Leave him in the house while you walk the dogs around the block, even though it is early afternoon, your usual work time. Keep his hyper little dog on a leash despite his protests because she will chase bikes, snap at joggers, roll in unspeakable things, and snoop in every gutter for garbage. When you get home, you will find him on the floor in the living room kneeling in front of the liquor cabinet in shambles. Without missing a beat he will say, "Pat! Where do you keep the tarragon?"

Lead him to the spice rack in the kitchen and locate the spices he needs. Watch as he marinates the squabs and himself in a mixture of melted butter, soy sauce, and herbs.

Offer to read aloud a story you've written about him for a radio broadcast. It is called "Cook a Turkey, Be a Man." Between the lines of his Thanksgiving recipe are all the reasons you hate and love him. You hope it will be a way to reconnect.

Don't be alarmed when he grabs the pages from you as you read the stuffing ingredients. You have added Italian sausage. He NEVER uses sausage. Not any. Never has. "Where did you get such a TERRIBLE idea?" You must correct it on the spot. And change the cornbread to Pepperidge Farm seasoned bread cubes. And delete the chestnuts. Add apple instead. And phone the radio station right away to make sure they don't air the wrong version.

He goes outside for a recovery smoke, collapsing in a chair on the deck in a shriveled heap, tremulous and lavender. It is only five in the afternoon. Two hours 'til dinner and no cable TV or vodka, but at least the network news will be on soon. The cigarette pinks him up a little.

"Don't you have anything to drink?" he calls out. "Some wine?"

We don't acknowledge vodka.

Go to the cellar to root around for wine. Everything is torn apart, which he cannot appreciate. Workmen have discovered dry rot while attending to another repair, and unseasonal rains have slowed their progress. Your father cannot see that a heavy door panel and an uprooted toilet block your way to the cellar door that closes off a crawl space where you once stored some wine. You break through like a coal miner and grope in the damp dark mud above a waist-high retaining wall for a bottle lying on its side. You find it and reappear in the kitchen none too soon. He is pacing beside the counter asking where you've been so long.

The wine, whose label long ago dissolved in the mud, turns out to be a good one. Sing to the dogs! The ditty about "A Froggie Would A-Wooing Go," then "Fiddle dee dee, fiddle dee dee, the fly has married the bumble bee." And last of all, "I Had a Little Doggie Who Used to Sit and Beg, but Doggie Tumbled Down the Stairs and Broke his Little Leg . . ." Get the dogs in a frenzy, jumping and barking. It is a party, after all. Turn up the volume on the TV news so Tom Brokaw can join the fun.

"Don't forget to preheat the oven and start the wild rice. And where's the wine? More wine! (Don't you want some?)"

Pour on the praise. No one cooks squab as well as he does. Or turkey or steak or lamb.

"Look at those poor refugees, those bombs. It's a fuckin' fiasco, a humanitarian disaster. Goddamn Milosevic. Goddamn NATO. Goddamn, the rice is burning! I can smell it! Didn't you turn down the flame? Add water quick. Hurry up. You women drive me crazy."

After dinner, fade fast to bedtime. By nine o'clock he's gone upstairs to his room. You go in to kiss him good night, but he's not there. His cane lies across the foot of the bed, where Sweetie dog pants expectantly. On the nightstand his pinky brown hearing aids lie curled on their sides like hermit crabs yanked from their shells. His teeth soaking in a glass smile jauntily back at you.

Ha, ha, they say, your house, your rules do not apply to him. It is understood. He has locked himself in the bathroom where he is sneaking his last smoke of the evening. No use playing cranky dorm mother and confronting him. Instead, go to the bathroom door and knock. Then shout as loudly as you can, "Good night, Dad. I just came in to say good night." Maybe he'll hear you, and maybe he won't. Either way won't make a difference.

Does It Match?

A blind man is waiting at a traffic signal to get across a busy intersection in Miami Beach. He senses a woman standing near him and turns to her.

"Pardon me, Miss, but I am vondering if you could please help me. I've been blind since birth."

"Certainly," says the woman.

"Ach, you are very kind. It is hard not being able to see. Such a challenge just getting dressed every day. Could you tell me, please, does my jacket match the pants?"

"Well, the jacket is green. The pants are red plaid. No, not a good match. And the jacket has some schmutz on the lapel."

"Oh, tank you, Madame, for telling me. I vould never know. Ach, and ze shirt?"

"Well, the shirt is blue and gray plaid, not a good match."

"Oy. And ze socks?"

"Well, you've got brown stripes on the left and maroon and yellow argyle on the right."

"Oh, dear, zis is terrible, but tank you for being so honest. Tell me, is zere anyting else zat doesn't match?"

"Well, to tell you the truth, you can drop the Jewish accent. You're a shvartzer."

Aloha Oy!

June 2, 1999

Getting into an unfamiliar rental car with Dad is life threatening. His hell breaks loose over any discomfort or dislocation, especially entering a car that has been parked in the noon sun at Kahului Airport on Maui.

In an attempt to head off a bad scene, Ron, already in Maui with his windsurfing friends, has picked up our rental car and parked it in the handicapped zone nearest the baggage-claim area. He wants to spare Dad the wait in lines for the shuttle and the car rental, which surely would have sent him beyond the boiling point.

Then Ron makes it to the airport gate with a courtesy wheelchair just as we disembark. Tanned and euphoric after three epic days of sailing and wave jumping, Ron bestows leis upon each of us and wheels Dad faster than an ambulance to the street curb for a cigarette.

By the time Mom and I show up with the luggage, Dad has finished three cigarettes and is fuming.

"What took you so long?"

"They lost Mom's suitcase, but it's coming on a later flight and will be delivered to our condo."

"Well, let's get out of here. It's hot."

Ron opens the car doors for Mom and Dad and hands me the keys.

From inside the car there is loud panic.

"Hey, it's an oven in here. You're killing us. Come on!"

I slide into the driver's seat beside Dad whose nervous hands flutter about the dashboard testing every button and switch.

"Goddamnit! Don't you have air-conditioning? Where's the fan? The vents? The window opener? I can't see a fuckin' thing."

Before I can figure out the dials, everything is on: the air conditioner, the blower, the heat, the defrost, the radio, the emergency blinkers, the recycled air, the map lights, the door locks—everything except the seatbelt, which he doesn't like to wear.

Instead of finding the brake release, I manage to pop open the hood and the trunk.

"Pat, you fool! What are you doing? Get out of here! Hurry up!"

After closing the hood and trunk, I start off quickly, hoping the motion of the car will quiet him. Dad wants to know where we are going. Why haven't I read the map? When Mom reads a road sign aloud, he bellows, "Shut up, Carol, you don't know a thing. Jesus, where are we?"

"Dad, don't talk to Mom or anyone else like that. I won't go another inch until you do better."

I pull over onto the rough shoulder of the road, stop, and search for my prescription dark glasses. When Dad's obscenities subside to a whisper and he stops kicking the underside of the glove compartment, I wedge our little compact into bumper-to-bumper traffic heading south through six-way stoplights.

Once the cars start moving, Dad leans forward in the plush velour seat, ready to navigate. Though he's never been to Maui, Dad comments constantly on the geography.

"We're driving north."

"No, Dad, we're going south away from the airport."

"Aren't we on the road to Wailea? It's north."

"No, south. The afternoon sun's on your right—that's west. Haleakala rises to your left—that's east."

It is hard to know what a person with advancing macular degeneration can see. The deterioration often takes years. Loss of central vision does not dim remembered vision or peripheral vision—or the wish to be in charge no matter what. Dad prides himself on his sharp sense of direction and still is a superb and stubborn navigator. Navigating compensates a little for not being able to drive anymore. It's one of the few opportunities left to prove he's always right.

The traffic stops again at a long light where three highways converge.

"Where did you say is Haleakala?"

"It's still east, to your left."

"Does that road go to Hana?" he asks, pointing to the right.

"No, the opposite. The one you're pointing to goes to Lahaina. That other one, to the left, goes to Hana."

"I don't get it," he growls, rummaging through his pockets for a cigarette. "Oh, no. I'm out of smokes. Stop at Longs or Safeway. I need emery boards, too."

"Later," I say, "let's get to the condo first." I assure him that Maui is the land of 7-11 and Kmart.

"No, Safeway's best, then Longs. Forget 7-11."

I promise to stop at a Safeway if we pass one on the way. Appeased, Dad fiddles with the window mechanism and whistles "Dixie" through his teeth. Mom, in her back seat, finishes the *Chronicle*'s crossword puzzle. I hum, "Take my hand, I'm a stranger in paradise."

"These are the worst seats," says Dad. "How can I adjust the tilt?"

He raises a lever and slides backward into Mom's knees.

"Ouch, Henry!"

Then he finds another switch that folds the back of his seat forward. Seeing him sandwiched between the two plush jaws of his seat makes me smile, and I veer into the right lane across lane divider bumps.

"Keep your eyes on the road! You're going to kill us all."

"Henry, stop!" shouts Mom.

"Me stop? She's the driver. Fool." He continues to adjust the seat levers until he finds a better position. "Jesus, I need a smoke."

"Want some water or gum?"

"Can't chew gum. Dentures."

My left hand rummages through my purse and finds a tin of Grether's blackcurrant pastilles.

"Oh, I love these!"

"Me, too," says Mom from the back seat. They momentarily turn into contented children. Dad's pastille gets stuck on the roof of his dentures. He removes them and pries off the gummy chew with his house key.

Mom and Dad make a pact when they travel that Dad will not drink. Suddenly weaned, he turns lavender-blue. He trembles and lurches. When I offer him my hand, he swats me away. Undeterred and dutiful as a guide dog, I walk a few paces in front of him, alerting him to possible dangers: "Three steps coming up, hand rail on the left. Wet pavement, then another step. Turn to the left. Large planter on your right."

"I can see, I can see," he says. "Get out of my way and shut up. I have my cane."

If for a moment my attention strays and I stop playing guide dog, he sets out in a wrong direction at surprising speed and panics, "PAT! PAT! GODDAMNIT WHERE ARE YOU? IS THIS ANY WAY TO TREAT A BLIND MAN?"

The worst is losing Dad in the aisles of Star Market or of Longs Drugs, where we go daily. Each morning a new urgent need arises: bacon, paper towels, Dr. Scholl's toe pads, a decent kitchen knife, a visor for under five dollars (never found), American coffee ("not that French roast shit!"), a San Francisco *Chronicle* for Mom, and, most necessary of all, size 13 hearing-aid batteries.

These shopping expeditions are the high point of his day. Each time we drive north to the malls in Kihei, he half asserts, "We're going south?" and I review the geography lesson with growing incredulity. I ask him to imagine a pie with the southwest quadrant missing. That is the shape of Maui. We are staying down near the southern tip where the pie's been cut.

For the first time Dad is never right. In fact, he is consistently, persistently wrong. How can I not be getting through, I who had once taught remedial reading? Without his bearings Dad cannot score a single navigational coup. He has no way to ameliorate his mounting discomfort.

Before I finish parking and locking the car in the Star Market lot, Dad's already steadying himself with a shopping cart and streaking for the entrance. Once inside he becomes disoriented and dizzy.

"PAT! PAT! WHERE ARE THE PHARMACEUTICALS? THE HOUSEWARES? WHERE ARE YOU GODDAMNIT? I CAN'T SEE A THING. YOU CAN'T JUST RUN OFF AND LEAVE A BLIND MAN."

Sometimes he doesn't know he's lost. We stroll up and down the aisles, and something in the towers of merchandise catches my eye. I let him wander off, and when I look up a moment later, he's gone without a trace. I run to the front or back of the store and chase silently down the crowded aisles. It's useless to call out because he won't hear. Most of the time I have the good luck to spot him before he misses me. Store personnel are quick to size up my predicament.

"Are you looking for the elderly man in a plaid shirt? He was over in Dairy."

Sometimes Dad simply leaves the store and returns to the car, which he finds with much more accuracy than I can. Mall parking lots teem with identical white rental cars, but he always finds ours and often manages to jimmy his hand through a window opening to unlock the door.

When Mom and I take excursions to the fancy resorts later in the day, we settle Dad and his cigarettes in the palatial open-air lobbies. Never still for long, he finds his way to the men's room or to a different cluster of mammoth sofas and armchairs, where we usually manage to retrieve him. But once, at the Grand Wailea, we return from a brief exploration to find a hotel manager mistaking Dad for a missing senile guest who had wandered away from an emergency medical clinic. We claim Dad just as the manager is trying to cart him off.

"What, what?" says Dad, adjusting his hearing aid. "What's he trying to do? Where's he taking me? "

"He thought you were someone else, an old man who's supposed to be in the medical clinic. But you're our geezer, unless you want us to have you committed."

Dad and I laugh long and hard at the bleak joke.

"Oh, Patchy," he wheezes, "it's the shits."

By evening, we arrive for pretentious hotel dinners in a frazzled state, all of us needing sustenance far beyond the scope of the menu. If waiters fail to flock around us like emergency room personnel, Dad launches into a torrent of demands:

"Where's my fork? My napkin? No, not the menu. Take it away, I can't see a thing. But I know what I want. Is there steak? New York cut, medium rare, with Bearnaise sauce. No Bearnaise? Do they have any A-1 and horseradish? I'll make my own sauce. Where's our waiter? I want to order."

Once the food arrives, Dad, who can't find what's on his own plate, never fails to comment about what is on ours.

"That's the most disgusting pile of food I ever saw. Yuck. Not *comme il faut*. You don't overload a plate like that. Is that ono or mahi-mahi? I hate warm-water fish. You can't get good fish in the tropics."

Once while Mom is cutting his meat, he sees her sneak a bite.

135

"You're taking food from a blind man! I saw you! How could you?"

Sometimes I interrupt his crescendo of complaints with a request to turn down the volume so Mom and I can enjoy our food. But if he detects a trace amount of garlic, which to him is an irritant more powerful than pepper spray, he rampages like a gored bull, rising from the table with a roar, and rushes outside to smoke.

By the end of dinner, he snorts and paws around for the bill, more irritable than he was on arrival. Surrounding diners are enjoying themselves too loudly, and the crooning guitarist is playing his unforgivable Hawaiian repertoire. Dad rises from his chair, tosses his Visa card at me, and rushes away, saying, "Tip fifteen dollars, that's five dollars a piece—and not a cent more."

When the check comes, I overtip, lavishly.

Dad's new tipping policy becomes a bone of contention.

"You mean to say you'd include an expensive bottle of wine in calculating a tip?" he asks.

"Of course."

"That's ridiculous. The wine is overpriced."

"Then don't order it."

"You don't know what you're talking about. If your mother ordered truffles, would you include that in the tip?"

"Of course. Those are the rules."

"Bullshit."

"Then don't go to such pricey places."

"I'd rather not."

"Good, me too. All the misery money can buy."

"It's your mother's fault."

"Oh Dad, drop it."

"No, you're the one who won't drop it."

Several days after getting home from Hawaii, Dad phones to thank me for putting up with him all week. This was as close to an apology as he has ever come.

"I should thank you," I say. "You treated."

"No, I was bad company. I get so frustrated with all my physical ailments. I mostly hate not being able to see."

And then he tells me that he'd had the map upside down.

"What map?" I ask.

"You know, the map of Maui."

In the weeks before the trip, he'd been memorizing the map of Maui on the overhead magnifier in his study. He knew the names of the main towns and tourist landmarks. He'd traced the contours of the coastline and committed every main road to memory. But he'd learned it upside down.

Swept Away

Hannah Goldberg *is sitting with her little grandson Morrie on the beach in front of the Fountainebleau Hotel on Miami Beach. He is digging in the sand with his little shovel when suddenly comes a huge wave and sweeps him away.*

Hannah struggles to her feet and shakes her fist at the sky.

"Gott in Himmel, how could You do this? How could You take my baby grandson from me? My dear Sheldon gives a fortune to the Federation every year. I demand that You bring little Morrie back! Right now!"

The clouds part. A beam of light shines down from heaven. A little wave appears carrying her beautiful boy back to shore and places him at her feet in perfect condition with the little shovel still in his hand.

Hannah looks up at the heavens and says, "The hat! He had a hat!"

Baalshamin to the Rescue

December 7, 1999

While I am Christmas shopping at Tail of the Yak in Berkeley, a sweet, trilling bird song lures me to the back of the store. There, in a tiny bamboo birdcage, is a wind-up bird with bright yellow feathers. I pick up the toy, turn the key on its underside, and watch transfixed as the little bird bobs on its perch and sings its cheerful song. "High-low, high-low, high-low, hi-hi-hi-hi-hi-hi! High-low!" It is Baalshamin! Made in China for only eleven dollars.

I buy the priceless treasure and drive straight into the city to give it to Dad. I can't wait for Christmas to come for fear he might die before then and deprive me of this blessed opportunity.

"Dad, it's me. Turn off the TV. I have a present for you."

"What, me? Why now?"

"You'll see. It's Christmas early."

He handles the package before unwrapping it, then holds the cage up to the light and squints at it.

"What's this? I can't see. It's a cage?"

I tell him to wind up the key underneath. I watch his face as Baalshamin bursts into song. A huge smile of recognition spreads across it.

"My God! It's that bird from your dream. What's his name?"

139

"Baalshamin." And I tell him the dream again for the hundredth time. Of course, it's a story he adores. He's at the heart of it, and it's the only way left to tell him I love him.

In the days that follow, Dad phones often, usually three or four times when I am in the middle of cooking dinner. He tells me how much he plays with Baalshamin.

"Whenever I feel low, I just let him chirp away with his head bobbing and his tail fluttering. It's such a cheerful song. And he doesn't shit. That's the best part."

I hang up smiling.

After dinner, I thumb through Leo Rosten's *The Joys of Yiddish*. Dad has loaned it to me knowing I'm transcribing his stories. He wants me to check my spelling.

I've always been curious about the name Baalshamin, which appears so clearly and insistently in my dream. I open the book to the B listings. The very first entry is Baal Shem, the name "given to saintly men who were believed to be endowed with mystical and healing powers, which they attained (it was claimed) through manipulations of God's Name." The most famous of the Baal Shems was Baal Shem Tov (rhymes with dove!), who lived from 1700 to 1760.

I phone Dad and read to him about Baal Shem Tov. He was "an itinerant evangelist, a mystic, an ecstatic, a poet. He preached in simple language . . . [and] told his followers to laugh, to sing, to dance in adoration of the Holy One—which scandalized the traditionalists." While the other Baal Shems were steeped in mysticism, numerology, and the abracadabra of rearranging God's names, Baal Shem Tov preached a down-to-earth gospel extolling joy and the enjoyment of life.

"That's right," says Dad. "Now that's enough. My hearing aids are going off. But read that book. It has everything you'll ever want to know."

Exodus Dream

December 9, 1999

Mom, Dad, Peter and Bev, Ron and I have been vaca-
tioning at a summer resort on a sandy shore resembling
New England's Cape Cod. Although we are supposed to
check out today, we are uncharacteristically relaxed. None
of us has started to pack. Books and magazines litter the
cabin. Wet towels lie on the floor. We've tracked in sand
everywhere. Beds are unmade.

It is bright and sunny outside. People of all ages are
assembling and walking toward the beach. We join them,
happy to leave our mess behind. It is warm and balmy,
and we are comfortable in our flimsy cotton shirts, shorts,
and flip-flops.

I fall in among some children, none I know, but they
are exuberant and friendly. We start to skip and sing as we
go along. I notice a curly-haired, dark-eyed girl of three
who is trying to keep up. I slow down for her and start to
tell her stories as we catch up with the crowd. She listens
with captivating intensity.

I want to keep her amused so that she won't notice
how difficult the walk is becoming. We are climbing a
steep sand dune, which gives way under our feet. It's
grown hot, and progress is slow, but the little child keeps
smiling as I talk to her. I bend over so that we are at eye
level, and I say things in different accents. She laughs and

keeps going even though the throng jostles us as people hurry past. We are surrounded by a forest of legs that keep climbing and climbing.

I stand up to see where we are going. Just beyond, where the gigantic sand dune crests, the open ocean glints far below. In a few more steps we will be at the summit of a cliff that plummets a thousand feet down into the water. The sand will give way under our weight, and we will all be instantly killed.

I turn around and call to the others to follow. As the crowd changes direction, I find Dad groping blindly with his cane. Somehow, despite the steep, crumbling slope and his awkward, oversized shoes, he has made it all this way. He appears confused and tired but is smiling. I hook my arm through his and say we are going back down the hill, an easier route.

I describe the playful children, hoping to divert his attention from our plight and from the fact that I had forgotten all about him the whole way up. He has good reason to be angry, but his good humor persists. He is listening to me! He likes hearing about our games.

The whole time I am regaling him, a foreboding tells me the danger is not over. We must get down from this crumbling dune quickly, before a sudden, strong tsunami engulfs us from behind and swoops us out to sea. We could all drown—gulping, struggling deaths. Or perhaps the ground beneath our feet will open up. An earthquake would shake us loose, causing us to plunge backward into the sea or straight down into a deep crevice, where we will all be buried alive.

I look westward toward land to see where we are heading. From my vantage point, still high on the dune, I can see extensive lowlands. Beyond the beach lies a marsh with a lagoon to get around, then flat grasslands that reach to the edge of a dark forest way off in the distance. There is snow at the forest's edge, and all of the deciduous trees have lost their leaves. We are going straight into winter, and we are unprepared. In our cotton shorts and flip-flops we will freeze to death. I have not even brought our sweaters.

I keep urging Dad along, relieved that his blindness prevents him from seeing the dangers.

"Did you show them the one about the flying bird?" he asks, still thinking about amusing the children. He stops and stacks his hands together to demonstrate. His thumbs twirl on each side like bird wings.

"Yes, we did that. They liked it."

Summer is over. We are walking straight into winter, and I can't reverse it. The ground crumbles beneath our feet, and I can't change that. All I can do is march along with the teeming crowd, one step at a time, not knowing what's next. I make up rhymes, imitate bird walks and animal gaits—anything to keep Dad going. We strut along so gaily together: penguins and ostriches, kangaroos and bears, zebras and lorises—all the animals Dad used to lecture about when he was a docent at the zoo.

Dad's blue eyes brighten as if they are seeing. He raises his index finger to conduct and bursts into an old favorite:

> Fiddle-dee-dee, fiddle-dee-dee,
>   the fly has married the bumble bee.
> The bee, said she, live under my wing,
>   and you'll never know that I carry a sting.

> Fiddle-dee-dee, fiddle-dee-dee,
>> the fly has married the bumble bee!

Giggling children join in. Together we walk in lockstep toward the inevitable. Yet we can have so much fun along the way if we are entertaining. Each step can be filled with delight when we tell stories. *Tell a story that makes them laugh and cry, for God's sake, and don't bore them.*

Hanky Panky

May 8, 2000

"Patsy, we've got trouble . . ."

Mom phones at dinnertime, the day before her birthday.

"Your father has taken a terrible fall . . ."

My heart lurches to my throat. My hand squeezing the receiver feels suddenly cold. So this is it, I think.

"He's cut his head just terribly. There was blood all over, gushing from his head and wrist and dribbling down the sidewalk. He lay there unable to get up. Alex and I were afraid to move him."

"Where is he now?" I interrupt, imagining Dad in a crumpled heap on the sloping sidewalk in front of their house, curled in a fetal position, unconscious, his skull cracked open.

"Upstairs in the bedroom. Alex brought him home from the ER a half hour ago."

"When did this happen?"

"Sometime around three this afternoon, I guess. We waited and waited forever. The nurses were just awful. Your father was having a fit—"

"Wait, was he ever unconscious?"

"No."

Mom explains that Alex had driven Dad downtown to a restaurant bar for his regular Monday lunch with his friend, Lou.

"He must've taken a taxi home and stumbled getting out. His forehead hit the cobblestone sidewalk, judging from the jagged gash. His wrist and elbow are cut up, too.

"Alex says a nice, middle-aged lady rang the doorbell to summon help. She gave Henry Kleenex for his wounds. Alex ran upstairs to get me. The nice lady was gone by the time I got down there. I would have thanked her.

"I called an ambulance, which came right away and rushed Henry to an emergency room. Alex drove me in the car, and we waited with him for hours, pressing towels to his forehead.

"It kept bleeding and bleeding, and he was just miserable." Her voice rises with indignation. "He kept screaming and crying. He was in the most awful pain. He needed a cigarette, and the nurses weren't at all nice. They took their time, and—can you believe it?—they were telling me he's been drinking—they could smell it on his breath—and that I should get him to stop.

"I told them he was just eating lunch with a friend, and they kept asking, 'How much does he drink?'"

"So what did you tell them?"

"Nothing. How should I know whether he'd been drinking? But I can tell you it was humiliating, simply awful. Finally I'd had enough, and Alex drove me home.

"Now your father's sitting undressed in his chair in the dark, moaning. He won't go to bed. He says his ribs are killing him."

"Maybe they're cracked. Was an x-ray done?"

"No, he never told the doctor about his ribs. They just sewed up his head—sixteen stitches on his forehead from his hairline to his eyebrow. It looks awful, and I have to change this disgusting bandage twice a day and apply an antibiotic. Alex has yet to go to Walgreens to get the supplies."

While I listen, my conscience harangues me. A good daughter would rush to their side and show that she cares. I should be rousing the others and mobilizing them into action. Be *nice,* above all be *nice.* But instead I'm doing nothing except listening and trying to gauge the magnitude of the emergency. When other people's fathers crack their heads, they suffer strokes, paralysis, heart attacks, broken bones, or, at the very least, concussions. But Dad is coming through with only cuts and bruises. In the background I hear him groaning.

"My ribs, goddamnit. My ribs are killing me. Get Ron on the phone. I need a doctor. I need a painkiller. NOW!"

"What's he taking for pain?" I ask.

"I think we have some old Empirin."

"Mom, are you saying he came home from the hospital with nothing for pain?"

"That's right."

"I'll get Ron."

Dad's moaning drowns out her thanks.

Mom phones back an hour later, after Dad has finally gone to bed.

"The strangest thing happened while I was having dinner tonight. Alex called me to the phone, and it was that nice lady, the one who had come upon Dad lying on the sidewalk. She called to inquire how he was. I told her he was just lacerated and bruised, and thanked her for calling. After I hung up, it seemed strange that she knew the phone number, so I asked Alex.

"'Oh, that lady, she is not a stranger,' Alex said in that high, excited voice of his. 'She is the same one who came for dinner the time you were in Washington, D.C. Mr. Henry knows her. She drove him home from downtown in her car. Its passenger door was open. He must have fallen getting out.'

"'So there was no taxi?' I asked him.

"'No, I didn't see one. No, no taxi, just her car.'

"Can you believe it?" Mom asks. "Your father carrying on like this at his age and in his condition?"

"Amazing," I say. "What are you going to do?"

"I'm sleeping in your bedroom tonight, I can tell you that."

"Good for you." For the first time in sixty-one years Mom is taking action, and I feel the welcome flood of relief, comic relief.

"Have I got a story for you! It'll knock your socks off!" Mom says the next morning, her birthday. She's phoning to confirm plans to go to Fleur de Lys for a celebratory dinner. "Your father isn't up to it. He'll stay home."

"We'll stop by to see him when we pick you up," I say. "How's he doing?"

"Fine. Terrible. Tell Ron to bring more gauze. He can change the bandage. You won't believe my news."

The receiver clicks, and she's off, back on party mode with a full social calendar, juicy news, and the promise of a gourmet meal. Yesterday our *Titanic* was going down, but today we're on a roller coaster climbing, climbing to dizzy heights. I hang on tight.

I'm struck, upon arriving, at how well my parents look. Dad is clearly tired but not more ravaged than usual. Ron removes the bandage from his forehead. The edges of the wound have already started to heal. It is not swollen or discolored. If anything, Dad looks like he's had a facelift on one side. The skin is smooth and flat, with no wrinkles. The scar will shrink to a hair's width and won't be noticeable at all. He'll be able to raise one eyebrow higher than the other, an added enhancement.

"I'm a wreck," he says.

"Yes," I agree, "but a good-looking wreck."

"He's a wreck," Mom insists.

She is a confection in silk. I've given her a peach-colored haori jacket for her birthday, and it looks delicious with her lavender blouse and ivory pants. She wears a colorful Venetian glass necklace and huge Zuni rings. Tonight, brimming with untold news, she's aglow except for her flattened hair, which doesn't get done for two more days. She is eighty-three today but could pass for seventy.

Mom is especially happy tonight because Peter and Bev's son, Daniel, is joining us. The seating will work out right: boy, girl, boy, girl. Watching her flirt with Daniel, I realize how much it counts to be with a man. Nothing to Mom is more woeful than an unaccompanied woman. If she and I are alone, her face goes slack, a wordless exhaustion blankets her, and she sighs deep, guttural sighs. But when Ron or Daniel is present, she springs to life, her attentive, witty self.

No sooner are the six of us wedged into my station wagon than Mom announces the news:

"I caught your father in a lie. That woman was not a

stranger at all. I confronted him, and he admitted that it was Delphine, Lou's ex-girlfriend."

"Oh, so he was having lunch with her?" asks Peter.

"No, he was meeting Lou for lunch. Maybe she just drove him home, or maybe she went along, too."

"Why would she be there if she and Lou had broken up? Maybe there was no Lou."

"No, your father said he had a date with Lou."

"Mom, why do you believe him?" Peter persists. "You know the guy can't tell a truth."

"He usually eats with Lou."

"How do you know?"

Mom pauses, confused, then brightens with an idea. "I know! I'll phone Lou and ask him. Oh dear, but then if it gets back to your father, he'll be mad."

"What difference does that make?" says Peter. "He's always mad. What a bastard."

"I could phone her, I guess," says Mom, "but, no, she'd get mad."

"Why don't you tell Henry that Alex saw him having lunch with her?" asks Ron.

"But Alex didn't."

"You could say he did," I add, "just as a way of getting new information. It would be a trick question, a trap."

"No, I can't lie."

"Why not?" laughs Peter. "He does."

"No, I don't want to get Alex in trouble."

"Jesus, why would anyone want to have lunch with him?" asks Peter. "He must be paying her."

"Yes," says Ron. "She has to be doing it for money."

"It would have to be a lot to be worth her while," Peter says. His brow knits in a calculating frown. "Mom, have you noticed any unusual charges on the MasterCard? Or bank withdrawals? He must be putting her up in style."

"What are you talking about?" says Mom. "The point I am making is that he lied about the taxi. Delphine drove him home in her car. Period."

"Still, I think you should check your bank statements and MasterCard bills," says Peter as we march into the restaurant.

The room is oppressively opulent with a canopied cloth ceiling. Other diners sit silent as figures in a wax museum. Aproned waiters and busboys part like a flock of white geese as the maitre d' leads us to our candlelit table. The staff clusters round to ease us into our chairs.

Huge dinner plates with a minuscule *amuse-bouche* in the center are set before each of us. While I am noting that the doll-sized portion is perfect for Mom, I overhear her saying to Beverly, "I wish I'd made the reservation at Gary Danko. Critics say it's the number one."

The next evening Peter phones with a full report.

"I had to go over to the house because Mom couldn't get Henry out of the bathtub. He'd been soaking his bruises and didn't have the strength to stand up. Of course, they don't have any safety features in the bathroom, no bars to hold onto, not even a rubber mat for the tub. So I get there, and what a sight! Your father's lying all curled up and shriveled in the bottom of the empty tub like an old scorpion. I haul him out—he weighs nothing; I don't know why Mom couldn't budge him—and I put him to bed.

"Then Mom shows me the phone bill from last month. There were fourteen calls to an unfamiliar number in San

Mateo. She got Dad to confess that they were calls to an old girlfriend named Louise. Now he says it was Louise, not Delphine, who'd driven him home on Monday."

"So now Lou has morphed into Louise?" I ask. "I'll get the skinny on her tomorrow."

"How?"

"I'll ask."

"Would you? That would be great. You know I can't."

We know that Peter's morality rankles Dad.

"Did Mom seem upset?"

"No. She stayed in the sitting room, finishing her crossword puzzle in front of the TV."

"So who's the mystery woman?" I ask Dad over the phone the next day.

"Louise? I met her over forty years ago. She was very young then, only two years older than you, and very pretty. Still is. Her first husband taught her to fly, but he died after two or three years. She was very insecure. We had an affair from 1962 'til about 1965. Oh, Patchy, it's like a bad ten-cent novel."

"Were you in love?"

"Oh, I don't know. Your mother and I were married much too young. We were twenty-one. What did we know?"

"I mean you and Louise?"

"Your mother's very nosy. I don't know what satisfaction she got ferreting out all this. She thinks I'm a liar and a no-good S.O.B. None of this would have raised an eyebrow today."

"Dad, married is married. People might fool around much longer now before they get married . . ."

"Damn right. Anything goes. I never had a chance to fool around." Dad's voice rises. "Your mother has such an open mind when it comes to everyone else. She's such a liberal. It's okay for everyone else but not for me. This is women's shit."

"So what became of Louise?"

"She married again and divorced. We kept in touch off and on. But your mother doesn't let up. I wouldn't pursue something like that. Why would I want to know? All women are bitches, and all men are bastards; it's a law of nature. Once when I suspected your mother was making out with my college roommate, I let it go."

"But, Dad, that was before you were married."

"Well, I'm sorry you have such an ugly father. I'm worn out. Aw, shit, I'm hanging up." Click.

I phone Mom late in the day.

"So Lou is Delphine is Louise?" I ask.

"Yes," she says wearily.

"Do you care?"

"Not any more. When I first found out about Louise years ago, you were away at college. It almost killed me. Some nights he didn't come home. I was a mess. For two years I had the worst ulcer and all sorts of aches and pains. But I got through it. He promised to stop seeing her."

"Do you think she'd want him now?"

"She can have him."

"A perfect solution," I agree.

True Confession

Old Itzak Himmelstein walks into a Catholic church and enters the confessional.

"Forgive me, Father, for I have sinned."

"My son, what is your sin?"

"I am eighty-one years old, married nearly sixty years to Naomi. We have three children, eight grandchildren. Naomi is in Long Island babysitting this weekend, and I met these identical twin girls, twenty years old, with blonde ponytails, big identical tits, and skin that fits. We have sex all night long, the three of us!"

"Oh my, that is a great sin. When was your last confession?"

"I've never been to confession. I'm Jewish."

"Then why are you telling me?"

"Why am I telling you? I'm telling everyone!"

Mother, May I?

July 2000

> I awoke before the morning.
> I was happy all the day.
> I never said an ugly word,
> but smiled and stuck to play.
> —wrought 1917

The cross-stitched sampler is faded now, placed for eternity behind glass in a chipped wood frame. It was embroidered by Gaggy on the occasion of Mom's birth and hung in her childhood bedroom, silently instilling its message.

I hardly notice that Mom is retreating back to the quiet industry of her childhood, so softly is she slipping from view. Her spirit has sprung a slow leak, but it will be months before we pay full attention. Coincidentally, her lifelong internist has retired, and she does not relate to the one Ron and I have found for her.

When I ask how she likes her new doctor, Mom says, "I forget his name. I think it starts with a G . . ."

"G—God awful!" says Dad. He is more petulant than ever since his fall. Topping his list of irritants is Alex's voice.

"Oh, Meester Seenton, Sweetie she won' come wit me . . ." Dad mimics Alex's high pitch and garbled diction. Dad's badgering has not produced the desired result, so now he turns to Mom to do his bidding, something she becomes adept at avoiding.

She is particularly resistant to the afternoon mail call, a high point between Dad's lunchtime vodka and the evening cocktail hour. He paces while she sifts through the pile and reads to him. To shorten the task she throws away as much junk mail as quickly and furtively as she can. Sometimes business envelopes fall into the wastebasket unopened.

"Carol, what did you just throw away?"

"Nothing, Henry. It's junk."

"Look, this is a business envelope. Open it and read it to me. So help me, Carol, you utz me."

Recently, a disturbing matter came to light. Mom and Dad's long-term care insurance has been cancelled. Mom is the culprit. She probably tossed out an overdue notice. By the time the lapsed payment came to Dad's attention, the policy had already been cancelled. His late payment was rejected. There is no recourse. I try for four months to get the policy reinstated. Twenty-three years of payments totaling $17,000 go for naught. A local TV station runs our sad story as a cautionary tale. Dad buries his head in his hands.

"Someday I'm going to kill your mother."

"I worry about Mom," I say. "I think she's losing weight."

"Huh? She's losing more than that."

"You mean her mind?"

"Yeah, like her sister."

"I bet she thinks of that. I should go with her the next time she sees her doctor."

"Damn right."

"What if Mom dies first?"

"NO!" screams Dad. He jumps out of his armchair and runs from the room. "She'd never do that!"

A quiet gloom settles in. Mom steals into her dressing room, where she secretly smokes. She stares out the window at the relentless summer fog. It comes early this year. She logs the foul weather in her datebook: *no sun, no sun, some afternoon sun, no sun, no sun 'til 4, no sun, some afternoon, SUN, fog 'til 5, fog 'til 3, no sun, no sun . . .*

She writes private notes to herself and stuffs them far back in her dressing table drawer:

> *Past pleasures:*
> *Going out for dinner with friends*
> *Going to dinner parties*
> *Going out of town*
> *Traveling*
> *Being on a board & having meetings*
> *Being alone: no stress, no waiting on, no requests,*
>   *no angers*

She lists all the countries she has visited (thirty-two).

One note, written November 14, 1995, pierces my heart when I come upon it after she has been rushed to an emergency room, and I am ransacking her drawers to find her glaucoma medication:

> *It is finally (& years overdue) time to take action. H*
> *flies into rages nearly daily, can't be reasoned with,*
> *can't stop drinking, can't seek help & it gets worse &*

worse & dog cowers every evening at dinner & before.
He is totally unreasonable & in his own isolated world.
His depression prevents him from wanting to go out—
to movies, restaurants, or to be with people. I cannot
plan a vacation because it's too stressful to be with him.
He must see a doctor, face his problems, get some anti-
depressant drug & stop drinking. Otherwise he should
move out & live elsewhere—a separation.

Pluses if he goes:
Less stress
I would be invited out
Minuses:

Who would fix things when they break? I am
dependant on him for that, for automobile problems,
for driving on freeways and at nite.

I would have to get live-in help and someone who
drives. That someone would also take Sweetie out in
afternoon & do some errands. Problems like TV, pic-
ture hanging, etc. I'd get Peter.

Sonoma? I would sell it. Would miss garden, but
would re-do garden here.

Stop! This is no-man's-land. How dare I linger here?
Have I forgotten the lacerating critique that stopped
me in my tracks in 1962, my junior year at U.C. Berkeley? For fun I had enrolled in a creative writing seminar
taught by the esteemed poet Louis Simpson. He strutted
back and forth at the front of the small classroom, as he
lectured the dozen of us with words that were polished
jewels. For my first assignment I submitted a depiction of
the depressed mother of my Radcliffe College roommate.

I had scrutinized her life of silent deprivation while I was a guest at their vacation cabin in Maine.

The mother's sadness hung like moss. Her days appeared devoid of any interest. She rinsed eggs before she boiled them and oranges before she peeled them. When I went blueberry picking in the woods, she stalked silently after me, fearing rapists behind every tree. I'm certain my essay was no prize, but when our graded papers were returned to us a week later, mine had no grade. Instead, Louis Simpson had written one sentence across the top: "This topic is not worthy of a reader's attention." I was humiliated and demolished as an aspiring writer, but I was also determined to become a much better teacher than he.

For now Mom tries to confine her distress to the dresser drawer and to her weekly therapy appointments. She also secludes herself for long hours in my old bedroom, where with the help of two technical consultants she has installed a turquoise Macintosh desktop computer. She writes down all of her coaches' explanations, then recopies each instruction onto a separate index card, which she tapes to the wall. Every card bears a headline in red ink: TO START: press power button. TO GET ON INTERNET: click connect icon and make sure status reads connected. TO SEND E-MAIL . . . TO RECEIVE E-MAIL . . . TO DELETE . . . Her handwritten notes comprise an entire user's manual!

On her forays alone in cyberspace Mom discovers Epicurious, Tobiko Caviar, and travel websites that take her in one click to France and Italy. When she is not experiencing glitches, her computer delivers gratifications long deferred and revives her feisty wit. She sends volleys of e-mail to her grandchildren, and after 9/11, she refers to Dad as Bin Laden. Flickers of her former vitality brighten my computer screen:

12/11/01 I will ask Bin Laden if he wants a reader, but it takes five minutes to read him the mail—no problem . . . Al Anon is a thing of the past for me. You must realize that I occupy myself with so many things and have enough friends and wonderful children!

3/18/02 You are TOO nice to have made all those arrangements for my birthday and I am most appreciative. You must not do so much for me because it makes me feel incapable and I'll NOT do the same for you on your 85th birthday!

Lord Chumley in Sumatra

A couple of old brigadier generals are drinking whiskey at the Officers' Club in London and reminiscing over their glorious adventures in the Royal Fusiliers.

"Pity about poor, old Chumley," one says to the other.

"What do you mean?"

"Oh, didn't you hear? He was drummed out of the service."

"My God! Whatever for?"

"He left his post in Delhi, and they found him living in Sumatra with an orangutan."

"No! Was it male or female?"

"Female, of course! Nothing queer about old Chumley!"

Rolling Dice

September 2000

Mom firmly rejects my offer to accompany her to Dr. G. "I don't need you to patronize me."

In truth I'm relieved because I want to believe she can cope. I'm writing and editing *Sex, Death, and Other Distractions*, my third book with the Kensington Ladies Erotica Society. Even though I don't discover Mom's drawer of secret ruminations until after the book comes out in 2002, Peter and I observe her with increasing concern. We speak by phone daily, but always Dad commandeers our attention away from Mom.

Another operation, more serious than the last, removes blockages from the femoral artery in his leg. While he is hospitalized for six days over Labor Day weekend, the hospital is understaffed, and his records are lost. Dad remains uncharacteristically calm and stoical. Peter and I take turns being with him.

I am surprised to find myself enjoying my hospital visits. Dad is a different patient this time. He walks up and down the halls all wired up to his IV antibiotics dispenser. Detoxed, he looks pink and refreshed. He listens and laughs at what I say and read to him. Even Alex visits voluntarily.

"Dad, why are you so tranquil this time?"

"I thought I was going to die."

The respite is short-lived. Once again Dad leaves the hospital AWOL to catch up on the bacon and vodka that he has missed. Refueled, he takes to stock trading more recklessly. Dad brags to us about his gains, never mentions his losses. On the sly, Peter meets with Dad's bookkeeper, estate lawyer, and brokers and puts together a timeline of Dad's trading activity. He charts both gains and losses. Puts and calls are the name of Dad's amped-up trading game.

"I'm not gambling. I'm speculating," he insists.

Peter sets up a family meeting to discuss finances. Mom won't come because money talk is strictly for men. Peter introduces the topic for discussion. Dad pretends to listen, then launches into a soliloquy, and runs out of the room:

"Now listen to me. I just want to say this: I know I'm blind, I'm deaf, I'm not as sharp as I used to be. So I've hired a money manager for your mother's account and our joint account. Couldn't I be allowed to play with the money I've made over the years on KLA-Tencor? Do let me play with my own money."

Peter and I are left staring at his empty chair.

Soon Peter unearths a new problem: a life insurance scheme on Mom's life. It will pay off handsomely if she dies before the age of ninety-one, but not a cent if she lives longer. We recoil from the idea and ask Ron to speak for us when we meet with Dad to discuss it.

Dad will listen to Ron, who is not afraid to stand up to him. Years ago in a resort dining room, with no provocation that we can remember, Dad had unleashed a barrage of imagined grievances against Ron. Ron quietly stood up, folded his napkin, and said, "Never talk to me again like that." Then he walked out. Dad never did cross that line with Ron a second time.

"Henry, we don't want to gamble on Carol's life or on yours," Ron says. "It's not right."

Without any drama Dad drops the idea. A crisis has been averted. Our talk returns to the topic of the moment, one that we all agree on: the election outcome of 2000. We are outraged that the Supreme Court has put a stop to the Florida vote recount and handed the presidency to Bush.

"Hail to the thief!"

"President Select!"

"This reminds me of the story of Moses Brown," says Dad:

On Election Day in Florida Moses Brown goes to vote.

The precinct captain asks him, "Do you know how to read"?

"Of course I do," says Moses Brown.

The precinct captain hands him a Chinese newspaper and says, "Can you read this?"

Moses Brown says, "Well, I can't read it word for word, but I can get the gist."

"So what does it say?" asks the precinct captain.

"It say Moses Brown ain't votin' in Florida today."

We laugh heartily. The joke is perfectly apropos.

"I can't die under a Bush," says Dad. "I'll have to live four more years."

"Four more years?" Peter and I chime in unison.

"Yes," says Dad. "I play a guessing game with myself. According to actuarial tables and taking my nature into account—my drinking and smoking and anger and will to live—I figure my life expectancy at age eighty-three years and ten and a half months is four more years, unfortunately for your mother."

Highway Robbery

One fine spring day Queen Elizabeth, the Queen Mother, and Princess Diana go for a drive in the country in their Rolls Royce limousine. While they are traveling a hilly lane not far from Blenheim Palace, suddenly four masked gunmen leap out from behind some shrubs and force the chauffeur to come to a full stop. Two of the gunmen order everyone out of the vehicle, while a third snatches the ladies' handbags. The fourth leaps into the drivers' seat, revs the motor, and as soon as his accomplices pile into the backseat, he speeds off.

"Oh, dear Mother, are you all right?" asks Queen Elizabeth breathlessly.

"Yes, dear, just a bit jostled," says the Queen Mother. "Actually, I'm quite relieved they didn't get my ivory brooch with the coral rosettes. I was able to stuff it in my vagina."

"Oh, Mother, that is splendid. I was able to save my diamond and sapphire engagement and wedding rings. I stuffed them in my vagina along with Great-Grandmum's gold watch. Diana, are you all right?"

"Oh, yes. I was able to stuff my diamond tiara in my vagina."

"Very good," says Queen Elizabeth. "That was clever."

"Pity Margaret wasn't here," says the Queen Mother. "We might have saved the Rolls."

Red Light, Green Light

November, 2001

At 2 Laurel we inch along with piecemeal improvements. A friend of Alex named Josie comes to help. She is smart and willing and quickly becomes Dad's favorite. He can find only two things wrong: she's a terrible cook, and she can't drive. But he likes her so much that he is determined to teach her himself.

Dad succeeds fabulously with the cooking. Josie writes every one of his favorite recipes in a schoolchild's lined composition notebook. In no time she masters shrimp cocktail, crab Louie, and hamburgers, each with the distinctive condiments that Dad requires. She advances to pickled pigs' feet, tripe Florentine, corned beef and cabbage, boiled tongue, and shrimp gumbo. She excels at cheese soufflés and popovers that are as light and high as Mom's used to be. Most important, Josie never fails to warm his breakfast and dinner plates. Instead of cowering in Dad's presence, Josie teases him and talks back.

"Sir Henry, if you act cranky, we won't have company for lunch. Who shall we invite today?"

Soon Josie runs the show. Her notebook bulges with the names and phone numbers of all Dad's doctors and the pharmacist. She spells out his medications and dosages. She records family and friends' phone numbers and birthdays. Under Dad's tutelage, she diagrams the family tree, records Dad's World War II experiences, and copies his recitations of weights, measures, and conversion factors.

"Your father is a very smart man. He teaches me so much."

The higher Josie soars on Dad's approval scale, the worse things get for Alex. A quarrel over the Thanksgiving turkey speeds Alex's downward spiral.

"Meester Sinton, how long do you cook an eighteen-pound turkey?"

"Three and a half to four hours."

"But the *New York Times* cookbook says six hours."

"WHAT? You're OUT of your mind. It'll be SAW-DUST!"

"That's what is says here on page—"

"Then why ask me, Fool? They're wrong, dead wrong. That's the most absurd thing I've ever heard. What a sure way to ruin a good bird."

"But Meester Sinton—"

"Shut up. Not another word. You've upset me."

A cigarette fails to calm him, so Dad grants himself extreme indulgence: he goes out with Alex to buy a car—a brand-new, metallic-taupe Nissan Maxima.

On the way home, desperate for another smoke, Dad's agitated hands grope the dashboard.

"Goddamnit, where's the cigarette lighter? I need it. Now."

"Meester Sinton, there isn't one."

"There has to be. You don't know what you're talking about."

When they get home, Alex reads the Maxima manual from cover to cover. The new models do not come equipped with cigarette lighters. Dad bellows at him some more, and for once Alex argues back.

"You're always blaming me. This has nothing to do with me."

"Stop whining. Your voice drives me nuts. I'll give you a thousand dollars to leave now."

"Fine."

And before Dad has climbed to the top of the stairs, Alex is out the door with suitcase in hand.

Shockwaves rattle the Bay Area. I get home from a busy day to a message machine bursting with indignation.

Dad: "Alex is a goddamn self-pitying crybaby. He takes everything I say literally. Now he's walked out, and your mother's beside herself. She won't listen to my side of the story."

Mom: "Your father has fired Alex. I don't know what I'm going to do. I need Alex to stay and Henry to go."

Dad: "Pat, where are you, damn it? Your mother treats me as if I'm a normal person. I am NOT a NORMAL PERSON! I've got to get out of here. If I were capable, I'd move out and take Sweetie with me. I'll go downstairs and live in Alex's room. Josie can take care of me and learn to drive."

For once I am ready! Armed with social service referrals, I phone Peter.

"The time has come to call the Jewish Family Service and work with a mediator. There has to be a way for Mom and Dad to live safely, whether together or apart. Maybe it would be good if you stay away so that Dad doesn't get sidetracked attacking you?"

Peter agrees and sets to work to find a face-saving way for Alex to come back. He succeeds by getting Mom to offer a lavish apology and a raise.

Forty-eight hours later Mom, Dad, and I embark on our first session around their dining room table with Craig Bruce, a social worker from the Jewish Family Service. I am giddy with worry and lack of sleep, having awakened numerous times to jot down agenda outlines, goals, and mollifying phrases. How will I get Dad to stay at the table when he has already announced his guidelines:

> I am going to make a statement and leave the room. I have a right to state my point. Your mother could do a lot to eliminate my shouting. She never hears me when I call. I need her to read to me, but she always says, "Later." She puts things away without telling me. That's no way to treat a blind man. I'm too fragile. I don't want to suffer. I can't live with her, and I can't live without her. I'll speak, and then whoever-he-is can take over. I'll go upstairs and come down after you've all had your say and dissected me.

Craig starts by asking Dad, "What do you want to come out of this meeting?"

"Not to have another."

The therapy session produces fallout. There is always an "afterwrath." Around nine the next evening my phone rings. Dad had gotten a splinter under his fingernail while trying to fix a door in Mom's dressing room.

"Your mother says, 'You don't have a splinter.' I blew my top and went and got a needle and tweezers. I had to use the TV magnifier. I was bleeding, infuriated. She says, 'You're impossible.' I took her by the shoulders and shoved her hard against a chair. At least get my side of it before you go huckle-de-buck for the police. I'm not too fond of your care today."

Police? Before I can respond, he hangs up. I am stunned. This is the first I have heard of physical abuse or of a police summons.

"I'm scared things are getting worse," says Mom when I reach her by phone. "This was a bad day."

After she reported the shoving incident to her therapist, the police and a social worker from Adult Protective Services came to the house to investigate. After questioning Dad, one police officer said to Mom, "I don't think you have too much to worry about," and they left.

Now Mom and I continue to attend therapy sessions with Craig, but Dad refuses.

"He's killing me with hand-wringing. He's an annoyance. Don't have him call me. He's the definition of a bore: someone who deprives you of solitude without providing company."

"Company"? We are off track!

"Dad, this isn't an entertainment. It's therapy so things can change."

"Fuck therapy. I don't think much of your mother's therapist either."

"Why? No change?"

"No, Carol's got a lot more backbone."

"You don't like backbone?"

"No!"

Business Fiasco

Poor Moishe Mendelbaum is distraught. After more than forty years in the dry goods business, he is going broke. He has lost a lot of money in the stock market and doesn't have the cash for a loan repayment.

"Oh, Bella, we are ruined. Business is bad, and I can't pay back a loan that is due tomorrow."

"How much do we need?" asks Bella.

"$10,000," says Moishe shaking his head.

Bella goes to the bedroom and comes back with a dress box crammed with $20 bills. She starts counting out $10,000.

"Bella, how did you get all that?"

"Well, Moishe, every time we had sex, I put $20 in the box."

"Oh, my God! If I'd known that, I'd have given you all my business!"

Masters of Deception

December 18, 2001

One week after the shoving incident, Mom's therapist phones.

"Pat, Henry punched her arm this morning, before drinking. He is escalating. Mental illness is very confusing—sane one minute and then a sudden flip. But it's those moments of rage that define what is happening. I think he has to be removed from the house. I am required to take protective action. I must report this to Social Services but want you to know first."

I dash to the city. Craig Bruce, Mom, and I are to have our third therapy session without Dad at 2 Laurel at three thirty in the afternoon. I hope our meeting will be well underway before the police arrive.

A scene of utter serenity greets me. Mom is puttering in the kitchen. Dad is upstairs in the TV room watching a *Dr. Phil* rerun. I've brought homemade toffee and a video of Mark Morris's Hard Nut ballet to keep him occupied while he boycotts our appointment in the dining room.

Craig Bruce arrives on time, followed by Jason, a social worker from Adult Protective Services. We huddle together around the dining room table as they lay out Mom's options in hushed, urgent voices.

"Another abusive incident so soon requires us to be here. There is a strong chance this could escalate. The police are on their way. You can request an EPO, an emergency protective order, that will remove him from the house and require him to stay away for a period of time."

"But where will he go?" asks Mom in a frightened voice.

"To a relative's house. To a motel."

"But there's not a place in the city that he won't get away from. He'll come right back home."

"And then, Mrs. Sinton, what will you do?" asks Craig.

"Why, I'll have to let him in. He'll be banging on the door."

"No, no. You don't have to answer the door," says Jason.

"He'll hammer down a door. He'll break a window." Mom's voice is rising. She is under attack. "There's no way I can keep him out."

"Then he can go to jail."

"Absolutely not. That's out of the question. It's a week before Christmas. I could never do that, especially not at Christmastime."

"Look, Mrs. Sinton. You have leverage now. But if you let him stay here, you have no options."

Mom sighs, shakes her head, and sinks her face into her beautifully manicured hands. "This is very hard for me. I'm not a warrior."

I am sitting in Dad's seat at the head of the table, shuffling through pages of notes about alcohol treatment programs. We scan the yellow pages for nearby hospitals' emergency numbers. All of us are scrambling for something—paper to write on, pens with ink, reading glasses, cell phones, and cordless extensions that work. Oh, why are batteries always dead at a time like this? Only Mom sits still and stunned at the center of our hurricane.

"I think Henry canceled an appointment with Dr. Wheelis today," she says. "Maybe we should call him?"

Dr. Wheelis was Mom's shrink for a time long ago. She reveres him. I manage to reach him at home, and he suggests three options.

"Your father is too feeble to go to jail. You can get him hospitalized as a psych emergency for two days of observation. You can install him in a hotel with a private nurse. Or he can go home with you."

I instantly and silently reject the third option. I'll be damned if I'll reward Dad with a holiday stay at our house. But taking him to Berkeley would make Mom feel safer. While the social workers try to persuade Mom to take action, I slip out of the room and phone Ron.

"Can you arrange to get Dad admitted tonight to Herrick Hospital's psych ward? I think it's the only way we can get him out of here and buy ourselves a little time."

"Sure," says Ron. "I'll get on it right away."

Two fresh-faced policemen have arrived and are being briefed by the social workers. All of them encircle Mom, beseeching her to sign the emergency protective order. No matter how persuasively they present the case, she will not.

Craig takes one of them aside and says, "I think we should talk to Mr. Sinton and proceed as if there is an EPO. He won't know. Pat, will you agree to take him to Berkeley?"

"Yes."

I rouse Dad from his lair upstairs, and he comes down with aplomb. He shakes hands with the officers and shows them to the living room. It is dark outside. I realize cocktails would have started hours ago. It is already after six. We have been at this for nearly three hours.

While I serve Perrier to all, the officers, seated on the brightly upholstered couch across from Dad, are explaining, "These days, sir, you can't shove or push or threaten to hit, not even in your own home. Verbal threats are considered abuse, too."

"Is that right?" says Dad, the clubby gentleman, sipping Perrier. "No swear words for dramatic effect?"

"Best not, sir, especially after APS has called us to your house twice in one week."

"Right now your choice, sir, is to come with us to jail or go home with your daughter. You cannot stay here."

"Then I will go with Pat."

"You may go and pack your bag. We will wait until you are in her custody."

"Would it be all right," I ask, "if I get us something to eat first? It's dinnertime."

The officers look questioningly at each other.

"We are supposed to wait until he leaves the house in your custody," says the taller officer, who glances at the massive wall of hardbound books. Has he ever been in a more sumptuous or serene living room? Then he adds, "I guess in this case we could grant some leniency if your father consents."

"Mr. Sinton, do you understand that once we deliver you to your daughter's custody, she is in charge?"

"Yes."

"Will you promise to do as she says?"

"Yessss," says Dad through clenched teeth. His eyes stare straight ahead and bulge defiantly, a signal no one except me fully comprehends. Taking on Dad alone is a risk, I know, but with my ordeal just beginning, I need to eat.

Dad goes upstairs to pack his overnight bag. I go downstairs to the front door with the social workers and the police.

"Best to keep your parents separated," the quieter officer says on his way out. "Don't let them eat in the same room."

I bring Mom from the dining room into the kitchen and seat her at the little pantry table where Peter and I used to eat liver and creamed corn on the nights she and Dad went out. Tonight she is the weary, beaten child.

"Once we get Dad settled in Berkeley, I'll let you know what's going on. Ron's looking for a treatment program. I want you to get some rest."

We are both dry-eyed and stony. Whatever feelings we once had seem to have atrophied. First I must feed Dad and get him to leave his house. Feelings and understanding are luxuries that will have to wait.

I bring a dinner tray to him in the living room.

"Take it away. I'm not hungry." He hunches deeper into his armchair and clutches the armrests to keep his hands from shaking. "I am NOT leaving this house without Sweetie. She is coming with me."

"Dad, you are in my custody. There is no negotiating. Tonight you are coming with me."

"I am not leaving this house without Sweetie."

"Dad, you heard what the police said. You agreed to the terms. Otherwise you're spending the night in jail."

"Fine, I'll go to jail."

"Dad, this is ridiculous. If I call, the police will be right back."

"Go ahead. I'm not leaving without Sweetie."

I go to the nearest telephone, just off the hall landing. I pick up the receiver but cannot bring myself to dial. Time to play the game his way.

"Dad, I can't send you to jail. I cannot do it. I'll pack up Sweetie's food and put her in the car. Then I'll come back for you. Here, I'll take your bag, too."

"Don't forget her pills. Or her bed. And her leash."

Sweetie follows me as I rustle around upstairs. Then I lead her by the leash to the pantry. I whisper to Mom to keep Sweetie quiet beside her until we've left. I give her some dog treats to use. Then I load Dad's satchel in my car.

"Okay. All set," I say as I return to the living room to get Dad.

"Is Sweetie in the car?"

"Yes."

I hand him his cane and lead him to the staircase. We go down each step in unison, one by one, then out through the front door into the cold, dark December night. Four more brick steps to the sidewalk, and I ease Dad into the passenger seat. I lock his door and dash around to the driver's seat.

"Sweetie! Sweetie! Where is Sweetie?" His hands are slicing through the air feeling for her at his feet and in the back seat.

"Goddamn it, Pat, you tricked me!" he screams as I gun the car through a sharp U-turn and up the three-tiered hill.

"Goddamn you! Goddamn you!" He tries to open his door, but I have the safety lock on. He kicks the glove compartment and pummels the dashboard. He tries to land a punch on me but misses. I zip down Bush Street, making all the lights. I don't think I exhale until we are past the anchorage and onto the Bay Bridge.

At this point Dad suddenly becomes accepting of his captivity. He picks his fingernails with anticipation. "I will sleep in Kate's room. I like her room best. Tomorrow I would like to go to the Oakland Museum. And what's that lunch spot I like, on the north side, where we eat upstairs?"

While Dad plans his itinerary, I say not a word. I will not be diverted from finding him a treatment program.

As we approach the house, Ron is coming out the front door. Before I reach a full stop, Dad is trying to open his passenger-side door.

"No, Henry," says Ron. "We're not staying here. I'm taking you to Herrick Hospital."

I hop in the back seat as Ron takes over the driving. For once Dad is speechless.

Bargain Cruise

Max and Moishe are wanting to take a trip while their wives go off to the Catskills for a mahjong tournament.

"I found just the thing!" says Max. "See this ad for a forty-dollar cruise from Naples to Solerno! Four days and three nights."

The two fly off to Naples and board the ship, which turns out to be a Roman galley. They are taken to their places in the hold below. There are twenty-five rows of benches, one bench for each oar. Each bench seats four rowers. A gangplank in the middle separates the rowers on the left from those on the right. Max and Moishe get seated next to each other and are chained to the bench.

A big black sailor in the stern starts beating on a drum while his companion struts up and down the gangplank counting time and snapping his twelve-foot whip at those who don't keep up. It is hot in the hold, and once or twice a day the whipper dowses the rowers with cold salt water.

Finally, on the fourth day, they reach their destination. As they are being released from their chains, Moishe turns to Max and asks, "How much should we tip the whipper?"

Deck the Halls

Christmas 2001

"Don't worry, I ain't suicidal," says Dad through clenched teeth as an admissions nurse removes his belt. "I can assure you of that."

For the rest of Dad's hospital stay, one of his hands must clutch the waistband of his pants to keep them up.

There are so many new doctors, nurses, and therapists to hear his story! But by morning the novelty has worn off.

"I've been up forever. I've gotta get out of here. This isn't punishment. It's torture. They're mean. Why I couldn't have come to your house I don't know. It's the shits."

Dad's confinement in the psych ward drags on for three days until we can negotiate a treatment plan. Finally, at daybreak on December 21, I come to take him to Oakland airport. We are flying to the Hemet Valley Recovery Center in Southern California. Hemet offers a treatment program "for the chemically dependent older adult." It requires a two-week hospitalization for detoxification, followed by a residential sobriety program.

Dad has consented to this on the condition that Sweetie will join him at the outpatient residence. Certainly Sweetie is as codependent as any of us! It has taken hours of negotiation to win this concession, both from the center's staff and from a very resistant Mom. A custody battle raged. Mom refused to be separated from Sweetie. Peter and I pleaded.

"We'll chauffeur her there ourselves. It will be only for three or four weeks."

Finally, the promise of a sober Henry won Mom over.

At the nursing station on the psych ward Dad's discharge papers are in order, but his belt has been lost. His free hand, the one without the cane, is still holding up his pants.

"We can't walk through airports like this," I tell one of the orderlies. "Please make him a belt out of something. Anything."

Just then a nurse comes running down the hall with his belt.

Seat-belted in our second-row seats on Southwest Airlines, Dad is agitating for something to eat before the plane has left the gate.

"I'm famished. I haven't eaten in days."

He has the window seat. I am in the middle, and a Jewish grandmother named Rose is on my right. She clucks approvingly as I unzip a small cooler and unwrap a tongue sandwich for Dad. I spread a napkin over his lap and hand him a half.

"Be careful, there's a toothpick holding it together."

"Good thing you told me. I could choke to death. What a way to lose your father. What can I put this on?"

"You can't use the food tray until we're airborne."

"I know that. Didn't you bring a plate? I need a plate."

"Just hand me the toothpick."

"Is there mustard? A pickle? I can't see."

He takes two big bites. I wipe a dribble of mayonnaise from his chin. The hand holding the sandwich is quivering. His right hand with the hospital ID band still affixed to the wrist gropes toward me.

"I need a drink. Something cold. Get the stewardess."

I retrieve a can of chilled lemonade from my cooler, open the pop-top, and hand it to him. Rose is impressed.

"You really love your father," she coos. "Such a nice man."

Yes, I want to say, *he hits my mother*.

Our trip is effortless compared to the Sturm und Drang of the last few days. In no time we are safely cocooned in a rental car heading for Hemet Valley Medical Center. Our freeway aims for Palm Springs. Dad presses his fingertips together and fantasizes about the excursions he will take, unaware that I will soon be turning off to get to Hemet.

"I will hire a driver for a day," Dad says happily. "Nana went to Palm Springs every winter. I want to see how it has changed and visit that nice oasis in a palm canyon. Remember? We took you there once."

We turn onto a two-lane road and continue south across a flat, brown plain with fallow fields on either side.

"My God, what is that stench?" says Dad.

In the distance I see clumps of white buildings in long, low rows.

"Chicken farms, I think."

"Shit. Chicken shit. It STINKS."

We are a long way from golf courses and manicured suburbs.

The polished, antiseptic reception area at the hospital masks the outside odor. While Dad is taken off to change into hospital wear, I give his chart and Ron's long, hand-written summary of his case to the director. Then I fill out countless forms as quickly as I can because I need to head back to Burbank airport before the afternoon rush hour.

When I finish, I go to the patients' day lounge to look for Dad to say good-bye. A sign on the wall says, "No men in women's rooms. No women in men's rooms." Another says, "The escalator to your recovery is broken. Please use the steps."

A group of male patients in baggy blue scrubs clusters in the middle of the room. The men huddle close and congenial like smokers in a bar, but they have neither cigarettes nor drinks. They are crowding intently, four and five deep, around a storyteller. It is Dad. As I approach, I overhear one man on the periphery of the circle say to another, "Things are going to be more interesting around here."

Dad is enacting the story about Max Shapiro and the tailor, an odd choice for this crowd, but one that best shows off both his Yiddish and his English accents. Wild laugher and applause break out as he delivers the punch line. I push my way through the men to give him a kiss good-bye.

"Dad, I have to go now . . . ," but he is already off on his next story.

Max Shapiro and the Tailor

Young Shapiro, who graduated Harvard at only sixteen, is now such a success on Wall Street that he treats his parents, Max and Rachel, to their first trip to London, all expenses paid.

"Today, Papa, I am taking you to Savile Row to buy a three-piece suit, made to order."

At the first appointment the tailor takes Max's measurements and shows him fabric samples. Finally, after three fittings, the suit is finished, and young Shapiro brings his father to try it on.

Max stands on a wooden pedestal before the three-way mirror. He fidgets with the knot of his tie.

"How do I look? Do I look English?" Max asks.

"No, not quite," says the tailor. "Try this."

The tailor tightens the tie and fastens a collar pin beneath the knot.

"Is this better?" asks Max, turning this way and that. "Do I look English?"

"Not quite," says the tailor. He places a black bowler on Max's head and inserts a crisply folded white hanky in the jacket's breast pocket.

"Now do I look English?" asks Max, gazing at himself in the mirror.

"Almost," says the tailor. He gets a black bumbershoot with a curved cane handle and hangs it from Max's left forearm. "There!"

Max stares at his reflection in the mirror. Tears start running down his cheek.

Young Shapiro says to his father, "Papa, what's wrong? You look great!"

Max wipes his eyes. "Such a pity we lost India!"

A Ghost from Christmas Past

I get home to Berkeley from Hemet at seven in the evening, barely in time to drive with Ron to San Francisco airport to pick up our son, Peter, who's flying in for Christmas. Just as we are leaving the house, the phone rings. I rush back to the kitchen to answer it.

A low, smoky woman's voice says, "Hello, Pat? This is Louise. You don't know who I am—"

"Oh, yes, Louise. I do. Dad has mentioned you."

"Well, I just got a call from him. He's been locked up in some treatment center in Southern California. He's going nuts. He's calling from a pay phone but has no more change. How are we going to get him out of there?"

I write "It's Louise!" on a piece of paper and motion Ron to go pick up Peter without me.

"So, Louise, what do you suggest?" I remember she can fly a plane and half expect her to suggest an airlift. "I know you and Dad go back a long way."

"Yes, forty years. When his life goes tits up, he calls me."

I pick up the pencil again and start taking notes.

"He called me at one in the morning last Tuesday. He said, 'I can't see you for lunch tomorrow.' He said something about a hospital. I thought Carol was in the hospital. Your father and I used to meet for lunch once a month. Lately, since all this trouble with your mother started, it's been every week. He tells me I'm the only person who will talk and listen to him. What's this about him being a threat? How could such a frail, old man be a threat? Ha, ha!"

Her laughter is deep and throaty.

"You know, I was the one who helped him when he fell down in front of the house last spring. I got everyone to come. No, he hadn't had anything to drink.

"Drunk? I've never seen him take more than one or two drinks. You can't pin it all on Henry. Verbal abuse goes both ways. Your mother wants out. She's dumb about this part. A divorce would cost at least a million dollars.

"He wants me to find him a place close to me in San Mateo. When I was very, very young, he helped me. He gave me money to go back to college. He was my mentor. Now, if I can help him in some way . . . he doesn't want to be a burden. Poor old goat.

"It's not nice for Carol to know he's been in touch with me all these years. Once we ran into you on the street in front of I. Magnin when you were twenty-two. I don't know if you remember. Henry always said, 'You'd like Pat if you met her.'

"He almost left your mother thirty years ago. He lived with me a couple of days. Then he got on his high horse and said in that puffed-up, righteous way of his, 'I have made a promise, a trust. (Ha, ha!) I will never break up the family. (More laughter.) We must stay together to preserve the estate. I have an obligation to my family and to future generations.' (Gasping for breath.) Oh, I really love that dear old gentleman. He has no sense of adventure. He can't go off on his own. He was outraged when Stanley left the family. I have always been a lifeline for him.

"What do I suggest? He's not going to be able to do this on his own. He could live downstairs at home, but he can't be alone. He would live with you. Or he could live near me with a dog and driver.

"Live with me? No, not with me. My condo's too small. Look, we all need people in our lives. I'm no longer a threat. I'm not the Other Woman. Pat, we are the strong ones."

The front door opens. Ron and Peter tiptoe in. I glance at my watch. I've been on the phone for an hour and a half.

"Well, Louise, let's wait 'til after the holiday and see how the Hemet program goes. Have a Merry Christmas."

One More Parrot Story

Mrs. Weinstein sees a sign in the pet shop window advertising a talking parrot for only ten dollars.

"Why are you selling him so cheap?" she asks the shopkeeper.

"Well, he grew up in a whore house, so sometimes his language is a little salty. But he's very tame and friendly."

Such a bargain Mrs. Weinstein can't resist. She buys the parrot and brings him home in a beautiful, new, covered cage.

She puts the cage in the front hall and removes the cover. The parrot looks at her and says, "Hello. New madam. New madam."

A couple of hours later her daughter comes home from school.

The parrot whistles a shrill "Woo woo!" and says, "Hello. New girl. New girl."

That evening just before dinner, her husband, Harry, comes home.

The parrot nods its head and says, "Hello, Harry."

Happily Never After

2002

The blizzard of faxes to and from Dad at Hemet subsides after only five days.

"Pat, you've got to get me out of here. I don't deserve this" changes to "I don't miss drink when I'm with people." He embraces his diagnosis: "I'm an alcoholic. That's as serious as being a diabetic. If I don't live by the rules, it could kill me."

Soon Dad is allowed to use the telephone.

"How do you know when an alcoholic is lying?" he asks me. "When his lips start moving."

Dad begins to notice the people around him.

"This is a great awakening. It's scary what's happened to the other patients here."

He tells me about his new friends and their tales of ruin. "Fortunately, I'm not as bad off."

On the sixth day of his confinement he leaves a message on Mom's answering machine declaring that he loves her.

He adapts to the regimented program, just like a good navy man.

"The hardest part is the listening. It drives me nuts, but I have to smile. There are meetings all the time and praying. We're forced to listen to books on tape, so I make believe I am and fall asleep.

"Precious is my case manager. She's very goyish and prissy. Today at a group meeting I told a joke: 'What is the difference between a vitamin and a hormone? Answer: You can't hear a vitamin.' People were very slow to laugh, but one by one they did, haltingly. Then Precious said, 'You're a very naughty old man.'"

Dad completes the hospitalization at Hemet in two weeks and is transferred to the residential treatment program. Peter and I keep our promise to drive Sweetie to him, but an accident on Highway 5 delays us. We don't get to Dad's group home until the middle of dinner.

The air in the overheated dining room is steamy with overcooked institutional fare. Eager to find Dad, I scan the room. There are five or six big round tables of diners, filled mostly with stooped, old women, many in wheelchairs. It looks like a terminal old-age ward, not a small group home for rehabilitation. A fake flower arrangement adorns each table. A grinning jack-o'-lantern of a man is waving his napkin at us. He is missing a front tooth. It's Dad! He rises from his chair and hobbles toward us as fast as he can to hug Sweetie.

Their joyous reunion blots out the misery of the accommodations. Dad leads us down a long hall to his shabby single room.

"Dad, where's your tooth?"

"I dropped my dentures. They broke. It fell out. Oh Sweetie, you're the finest dog in America!"

He settles back grimacing onto a lumpy little bed, and Sweetie jumps up beside him.

"Patchy, what's this?" he asks as he probes the mattress under his shoulder.

I pull back the bedding and see an exposed mattress coil springing up.

"Shit, Dad, this is terrible."

"Just look at the love in the dog's eyes!"

"Dad, are you all right?"

"Now I am. With my Sweetie here. I have a terrible kink in my upper back. Yes, there. I hurt it getting my suitcase down from a high shelf in the closet at the hospital. Did you bring her leash?"

"Yes, and her dishes and food. Here's a note from Mom reminding you to give her two pills a day. They're in this envelope. Will you be able to bring her to group meetings?"

"Damn right, so long as she doesn't bark or disturb anyone. Now Sweetie, you'd never do that, would you?"

Four days later Dad's case worker from Hemet phones to report that Sweetie has been barking, peeing on the carpet, and upsetting the other residents. She and Henry are expelled and must be picked up at once. We are instructed to get all liquor out of the house and to find a Jewish AA group for Dad. "And don't baby him."

Ron flies down to Southern California and rents a car to drive them home to San Francisco.

"They always blame the dog," says Dad when Ron arrives.

Dad never again drinks alcohol, which amazes all of us. He wears his diagnosis, alcoholism, like a badge of honor. The sharp pain in his back turns out to be a fractured vertebra. For a change he is willing to take medicine: ibuprofen for his back, quinine sulfate for his leg cramps,

195

even Paxil and Prozac to elevate his mood. His fling with antidepressants is brief. Most make him dizzy.

Dad's new sobriety is a curse for Mom. He no longer falls into postprandial slumbers. Instead, he lasers his wide-awake attention on her all day long and keeps score.

"She comes downstairs with her newspapers," he reports to me. "She's all avoidance. She's never once asked me about Hemet. There's no common ground, none. She hates me. I'll accept my faults, but she has yet to make an error. I can be just as angry with her sober as drunk."

His mood darkens further because Josie is not turning out to be a good driving student.

"I tell her, 'Josie, you are living a lie,'" a line he has picked up from TV therapist Dr. Phil. "'You pretend to want to learn to drive, but you are making no progress, none at all. Your fear of driving is not a phobia; it's a psychosis!'"

"Dad," I say, "this is very hard for Josie. She has told me how much she wants to please you, but once she was in a very bad car accident. Someone died. She really is afraid."

"Nonsense. Anyone who wants to can learn to drive."

"She doesn't really want to."

"That's what I mean. She's living a lie. I can't stand it. This house is fucked up for fair."

Jake the Tailor

Mr. Smith was a very successful businessman until the age of fifty-five, when he began to develop severe headaches. He consulted with doctors at the Mayo Clinic, but the headaches persisted. He visited a famous neurologist in London to no avail. No matter what he tried—acupuncture, hypnosis, painkillers, changes in diet—his chronic headaches never let up.

Finally after six years of suffering, Mr. Smith and his wife fly off to a renowned surgeon in Hong Kong.

The surgeon conducts many tests and concludes that he can guarantee Mr. Smith a complete cure, but it will require surgical removal of his testicles.

Mr. Smith and his wife carefully discuss the pros and cons over dinner. With so much of his life and accomplishments already behind him and only pain and suffering ahead, the Smiths opt for the surgery.

When Mr. Smith wakes up from the operation, he is so happy. His headache is gone. For the first time in six years he feels no pain. To celebrate, he takes his wife to London for a week of theater and sightseeing.

While he is there Mr. Smith decides to have a whole new set of clothes made for him by Jake the tailor on Savile Row.

"I want everything new, from head to toe," he says to Jake the tailor. "My hat size is—"

"No, don't tell me, I know," says Jake. "You're a 7 and 3/4."

"That's right!" says Mr. Smith. *"And my shirt size is—"*

"No, don't say it. You're a 15 / 33."

"Yes, exactly! And my jacket—"

"I know. Your jacket is 40 regular."

"Amazing," says Mr. Smith. *"And my pants?"*

"34/31."

"You're right again! And while we're at it, I'd like some new underwear. My underpants are—"

"Size 36."

"Aha! I finally got you. I've always worn a 34."

"Well, suit yourself," says Jake the tailor. *"Your size is 36. A 34 will squeeze your nuts and give you terrible headaches."*

911

September 2, 2002

When the phone call came, I was on my Monday morning hike in Tilden Park with my dear friend Linda and our dogs. Our ten-year ritual is well choreographed. Rain, shine, and once in snow Linda rolls by to collect us in her "barf buggy." The name refers to the eighteen months it took to subdue her dog Bonnie's car sickness.

Linda swings open the passenger-side door for Meeker, Lizzie's successor, and me and calls out, "Did anyone die? Did your mother finally spend the night?"

"No. She got the dates mixed up, but the strangest thing happened last Thursday night."

I'd been reading from *Sex, Death, and Other Distractions* with the Kensington Ladies at Booksmith in the Haight. My relatives were cautiously supportive of my fling with erotica. My brother, Peter, declared the writing "not bad for cliterature." This particular evening he and Bev had brought Mom and Auntie Marge to the reading, but it was so crowded they couldn't sit together. We'd planned to meet afterward for dinner, but while I was standing at the mike reading my story, "Viagra Blues," Mom stood up and started inching past all the seated people in her row. She disappeared out the front door into the night!

"Oh, no!" says Linda. "What did you do?"

"I had to keep reading. Luckily, Kate's friend Nicki was standing in the back of the throng and ran out after Mom."

"Did she disapprove of your story?"

"No, she was hungry and had forgotten our plan to go to a restaurant."

"So, what are you doing today, after our walk?" Linda asks.

"Bringing lunch to 2 Laurel. I didn't visit yesterday."

"You're a bad person."

"To the core," I agree. In truth, I'd had no excuse. Sunday is the day Mom and Dad have no help. Mom sounded tired when I phoned. Though it was nearly noon, she was just having breakfast. She said she didn't even feel like getting dressed. I offered (weakly) to bring dinner, but she said no, Alex had left something. She wasn't hungry anyway. More than anything I wanted to hoard a whole day at home with Ron. I took a pass and promised to bring lunch today, Monday.

The fog is lifting as Linda and I climb the Seaview Trail that traces the spine of the East Bay hills. On a clear day in winter we can see from the snowcapped Sierra in the east to the Farallon Islands in the west. Our talk strays to our children and to politics, and soon we are laughing and swearing and inciting the dogs to riot. They chase across a desiccated hillside where not even a stubborn foxtail has survived the summer drought. Everything is pulverized under foot. Gone are the golden grasses and late wildflowers. It's Labor Day, and already the poison oak has shed its reddened leaves. The trail, a gooey impasse during winter rains, is hard-packed now, with deep etchings of paw and hoof prints imbedded like fossils. This is as ugly and monochromatic as these hills get, but I think they're beautiful. I love them in their dusty autumn disarray as much as Linda loves neatly folded laundry.

Meeker backtracks toward me and circles around to present his rump for a pat, his form of thank you. He looks back at me over one shoulder and gives me a toothy, one-sided grin, a perfect Dick Cheney smile.

"Lovely Linda, you've given me a mood transplant. How can I thank you?"

I am so at ease when I get home that I forget to check the answering machine. A bubble of contentment surrounds me as I change clothes and scrounge up lunch fixings. I pack the car and back out of the garage. I hear the phone ringing but feel no urgency to stop and try to get it.

And then the bubble bursts. Ron runs out the front door.

"Your father phoned. Something happened to your mother at breakfast. She's conscious but not able to talk. They called 911, and an ambulance took her to the hospital. Alex and Josie are with her. Your father can't reach Peter or Bev. Maybe they're away? Page me when you know what's going on, and I'll come over after clinic."

I drive straight to Dad's. He shouldn't be alone, blind and deaf, especially not after such a scare. I'll give him lunch and get the story from him. Fate has struck Mom, but she is under the care of doctors while he is alone at home. Like a good planet, I remain in correct orbit circling his white-hot sun. His gravitational force is greater.

Defying Gravity

My parents' wind-whipped neighborhood has blossomed into full sun by the time I reach the house. The last traces of summer fog have vanished, and everything sparkles in gratitude. On the sidewalk outside the neighbor's eternal construction zone, the workmen's port-o-potty is the same blue as the noon sky. Leafy branches of the flowering pear trees hang still for a change, and mock orange releases its fragrance.

I enter through the garden gate because that is where I'd find Mom on a day like this. She'd be squatting in the dirt, wearing her mangled magenta straw hat, planting bulbs, or poking through roses to pick a bouquet of pinks, oranges, and reds. She's a lifelong gardener, as seduced by flowers as any bee, and her fresh arrangements enliven every room in the house.

Lately, she's had to rely more on a hired gardener, concentrating what's left of her energy on the container plants that crowd the deck off the dining room above. I climb the stairs to the deck garden. I picture her immersed in the daily crossword puzzle on the weathered chaise lounge. She'd be in her characteristic pose: knees bent to shoulder height with the folded newspaper pressed against the slope of her thighs. Today no one hears me coming. Bright geraniums, asters, verbena, and lobelia nearly obscure deaf Sweetie, who sleeps on the chaise with her tail unfurled. From the kitchen comes the whine of an eggbeater.

Dad is stooped over a bowl beside the stove whipping egg whites. He has peripheral vision only in the right eye. He cocks his head sideways, facing away from me. His better eye dips toward the mixing bowl. He bobs like a pecking pigeon. Bird analogies rush to my rescue for I cannot bear to see him as a stranded, stooped old man. Dad has managed to separate four eggs, more or less, with the yellows almost evenly divided between the counter top and an aluminum bowl and the whites mostly intact in the Pyrex bowl that's tilting toward the edge of the counter. A blue and orange flame blazes from the nearest front burner, tantalizingly close to his right elbow, while a frying pan with unmelted butter perches with its long handle at an odd angle atop an unlit burner. I reach out to turn down the flame.

"Don't touch anything! Can't you see I'm making *omelette aux fines herbes*?"

I back off and set the table for two in the dining room. I choose good forks—the ones that haven't got chewed up in the disposal yet—and the deluxe, double-ply paper napkins.

When the beating stops, I rejoin him in the kitchen. I hold my questions, for I know not to interrupt mid-omelette. Important things first: he is dumping quivering fistfuls of salt, pepper, and dried herbs into the bowl. Finally he sets the frying pan over the flaming burner. I watch with some concern as he folds the whites into the yellows, then slides the mixture into the frying pan. He wipes his hands on his powder-blue cashmere sweater, leaving slimy streaks of raw egg.

"Get the plates for me."

I reach to open the warmer above the top oven. New stoves do not have this feature. Both the stove and I were made in 1941. "Warm plates for warm food, *c'est comme il faut*," Dad insists.

Before the omelette has set, he is dishing it onto the heated plates. As I carry the runny portions to the table, I wonder if I will die of salmonella before he does.

"So what happened?" I ask once we are seated.

"I was upstairs getting dressed when Josie came and got me.

"'Sir Henry, something is wrong with Miss Carol,' he mimics her Tagalog accent. 'She dropped the newspapers on her way in to breakfast. Then she sat down at the table and couldn't speak or eat.'

"When I got downstairs, your mother was sitting at her place not moving. I told Josie to be sure her mouth was empty so she wouldn't choke and then call 911. They came immediately and took her to Pacific Medical."

"Was she conscious?"

"Oh yes."

"And able to sit here at the table? Didn't fall over or slump?"

"No. Nothing like that. Her hands were like this, perched on the table in front of her. Now go phone the hospital and see what's going on." His fork makes angry jabs at the plate, seeking out more omelette. Then he throws his napkin to the floor. "No one tells me anything."

The hospital connects me to the emergency room, where I am put on hold. I cradle the cordless phone between my ear and shoulder and swirl the raw omelette around with my fork. Dad lights a cigarette.

At last an attendant answers. Yes, my mother has been examined. No, they cannot give out her condition over the telephone. Yes, she will probably be admitted for at least one night. I report all this to Dad, then go to gather some things for her. I fold up the morning paper, careful to include the crossword puzzle. I search upstairs for her bed jacket, comb and brush, Dusty Rose lipstick and Sandalwood Beige powder. From her nightstand I scoop up the latest *New Yorker*.

I rummage through her dresser drawers looking for her three glaucoma medications. Instead I find torn scraps of paper with spidery scrawlings. Some are crosshatched tallies of cigarettes smoked daily: nine, seven, eight. One promises, "Tomorrow I will stop."

A haunting memory resurfaces: About a year ago, in a moment of rare revelation, Mom said to me, "I feel as though my whole life has been a failure."

Her confession caught me by surprise, and much to my later regret, I found myself unable to listen. My flood of words drove her back into silence.

"But, Ma, you've done so much. You became an artist with national recognition. You traveled everywhere. You had us. You kept the family together. No one can match your wit or taste and style . . ."

And then I said the very words she used to say to me when I was a weeping child: *No! Don't feel that way.* Those same awful, diminishing words that once rode roughshod over me and made me feel ashamed and failed and unlovable.

Mom tried to keep her suffering to herself, allowing us to pretend it wasn't killing her. Unable to bear her pain, I slam her dresser drawer shut and rush back downstairs to the dining room and to the invigoration of Dad's impulsive chaos. I clean up the lunch mess and leave Dad to his blaring television, promising to phone as soon as I know anything.

In the emergency room I find Mom lying on a gurney in a small examining room with Alex and Josie at one side. She is on her back, her head on a pillow. I hold her face in both my hands, the first time I have done such a thing since childhood. We search each other's faces. Her huge eyes are wide open and wondrous—the most breathtaking sapphire blue. No one I know has such dark blue eyes.

I search her face for clues. The moment is intensely private and invasive. What is she thinking? Feeling? Is she afraid? She gazes into my eyes. She is calm. The expression on her face is definitely not vacant. She looks bewildered. I am certain she knows who I am and where she is. She understands as well as I do that her body has betrayed her. I ask if anything hurts, and she shakes her head a slight no.

I hold her impeccably manicured hands. When I ask if she can squeeze mine, she responds with some pressure, more from her left hand than her right. Her hands are cool, and I ask if she is cold. And then she tries to speak. Her mouth opens, and her dark eyebrows knit in a deep furrow as she utters a throaty, "Nuh, nuh, n-n-n-oooooooooo . . ."

"No?"

She tries again, but the only sound she produces is "unh, unh, nuhhh." Her eyes flash exasperation.

Josie whispers, "She cannot talk or swallow. The doctor says she had a stroke on the left side."

A young woman doctor enters and explains in a clear voice what has happened. The language and delivery are completely value neutral and mechanical. The CAT scan showed an infarction in the left frontal lobe. There is a lesion about the size of a quarter, resulting in aphasia and some hemiplegia. Her elevated CPK indicates a possible mild heart attack. Since she can take nothing by mouth, they have started an intravenous line for fluids. A sonogram of the carotid arteries and an echocardiogram of the heart will be done, and a neurologist will see her after she is admitted. The doctor is calm and methodical. The language sounds foreign. No word or gesture summons any alarm. We could be discussing a plumbing or electrical problem. Mom and I sit there wide-eyed and attentive as if we comprehend. The doctor asks if I have her durable power of attorney. Does she have allergies to medications? For how long has she been losing weight?

"About a year," I say, and then ask, "What is her weight?"

"Seventy-seven pounds."

I suppress a gasp. Mom is not looking at us. Is she pretending not to hear, or has she not been following any of this?

The doctor tapes an NPO sign to the gurney and leaves.

Josie asks, "Pat, would it be all right if Alex and I go back to the house and have some breakfast."

"Sure. What time is it?"

"Two thirty."

"Oh my gosh, you've been here for hours."

We hug good-bye, and I pull up a chair beside the gurney. Anyone who has spent more than ten minutes in a hospital has shared the experience: first, the suspension of time. Under the harsh florescent lights, day and night become one. Other markers track time. Squeaky soled shoes signal the changing shifts of nurses. Meals roll by on delivery carts, leaving gravy-scented trails. Beeping watchdog machinery announces another clogged or empty line, and always the regular, rustling parade of orderlies taking "vitals" and doctors rounding early and late.

A nurse comes to take us upstairs to the medical floor. Mom frowns angrily when I tell her she is being admitted for the night.

"Nnnnnnnuh . . . nnnuuh . . . n-n-n-ooooooo!"

I explain that some tests need to be done. She rolls her eyeballs, and her mouth turns down. I know the look well: "This is the last place I want to be."

While Mom is being catheterized, I return to 2 Laurel to search for her medical directives and have a quick dinner with Dad and cousin Barbara. Barbara is Bobby's daughter and a trained nurse. She is six years younger than I and able to hold her own with anyone, even angry men, but she visibly blanches when Dad lights into me.

"Who's with your mother? What? You left her alone, unable to talk? How will she signal for help? Get up to pee? Why haven't you arranged for a private nurse? Why am I always the one to think of these things? What is wrong with you?"

I leave Dad with Barbara and rush back to the hospital to hire a night sitter. Peter is already there, and we stay late at Mom's bedside.

The next morning Mom submits to batteries of perception tests like a flunking schoolgirl. The speech therapist and occupational therapist speak to her in singsong voices. I turn away and busy myself making a photo collage to show Mom at her best. I want the staff to know who this trapped, silent wisp of a woman really is.

I stay at her bedside answering the phone. Friends send beautiful flowers and notes, which I read to her. She brightens when grandson Adam and his girlfriend, Eileen, visit, and she tries so hard to speak to them but can't. Cousins stop by and lift her spirits with nostalgic offerings. Joan reads from A.A. Milne's *When We Were Six*, Mom's childhood favorite. Margot has composed a letter from Rosebud, the Tahoe fairy who wrote to us at Rampart. I think she was Mom's invention, and I remember being told that when she wrote for humans, tiny Rosebud had to roller-skate over the paper while holding a normal-sized pencil upright like a log. Mom listens intently to these snippets from childhood. I think she understands.

I stop by 2 Laurel every evening to give Dad the daily report. His intensifying rumblings are growing too insistent to ignore. Three days into Mom's ordeal, he is clearly on the warpath, bracing for a showdown with Peter.

"That brother of yours drives me crazy. . . . He's being a goddamn Pollyanna. . . ." I dive in before he can launch a full-fledged attack.

"Dad, he's trying to be positive. He's doing the best he can right now."

"Oh, stop it. You always stand up for him. How do you think I feel?"

What Dad doesn't know, what neither of my parents know, is that Peter has been diagnosed with prostate cancer and is preparing for major surgery on October 15. All summer he has been exercising and dieting. He has eliminated dairy, fat, and sugar. Like a foraging bear, he eats fruit, berries, greens, and fish. He raids his beehives for honey and rides his bicycle daily to the beach and back.

As Peter's pounds melt away, the defining contours of his jaw and neck become visible beneath his trim white beard. Gradually, with the pillow of his torso receding, his belly flattens and no longer overhangs his belt. To reduce stress, he attends lectures, practices meditation, and keeps visits with Mom and Dad to a minimum. He smiles and laughs more than he has in years.

Throughout Mom's hospitalization, I wake in the dark before dawn with ideas for dealing with Dad. I hold back until daybreak before phoning Peter. Our conferences are quick. He gravitates to Mom, getting to the hospital in time for early medical rounds and monitoring her care and progress. I oversee Dad and the help and fill in for Peter at the hospital during the day. We usually overlap at night.

"Vesuvius is going to blow," I warn. "Would it be okay if I tell Dad your medical news to get him to back off?"

"Do you think it'll work?"

"Of course. How could it not?"

I wait until the next time Dad gets Peter in the cross-hairs. It happens the very next day, the fourth day of Mom's ordeal and the hardest yet. Though her condition appears to be deteriorating as she sinks more deeply into passivity, the hospital suddenly decides to transfer her to an intensive rehab program at the Ralph K. Davies Medical Center.

"Ralph K. Davies doesn't take just anybody," the caseworker says. "Your mother qualifies."

Peter and I look at each other dubiously. Mom's scores on the evaluation tests are rock bottom, but if Ralph K. Davies is the equivalent of Harvard for stroke patients, how can we deny her the opportunity?

I arrange for Mom's transfer and get her settled in a four-bed room. She looks around and closes her eyes, utterly dejected, despondent.

"Mom, you won't be here long. This is only for rehab until we can bring you home."

Mom doesn't react. My words sound hollow, untrue.

Leaving the Davies Medical Center with troubling thoughts, I go to Dad's for dinner, again with cousin Barbara. I expect to simplify for Dad the events of this long, unhappy day, but before Barbara and I have sat down, he starts in on Peter.

"Your goddamn brother! He's driving me crazy. Let me tell you what he did today . . ."

"Dad," I interrupt, "do you want to recite your list of grievances against Peter, or do you want some new information?"

Dad looks at me, startled. He eyes get beady and hard.

"New information," he says.

With a steady voice I tell Dad why Peter has been keeping his visits with him short and why he's been on a diet and exercise regimen.

"He has prostate cancer. It was detected very early. His operation will be October 15."

Dad looks at me with steely intent. He rises from his chair clenching his fists.

"How long has he known?"

"Since June."

"Who's his surgeon?"

"Peter Carroll, the best, at UCSF."

"And when did you say?"

"October 15."

And then, with the color rising in his face, he says in a high, tight voice, "He didn't tell me! He never told ME! HE EXCLUDED ME! I'll cut him off without a cent!"

"But, Dad, you and Mom have enough troubles. He was going to tell you closer to the operation. He was protecting you."

"OH BULLSHIT!" He spits out each word. I watch the spittle spray. The cords in his neck flex. "I'm his father, for God's sake. He never told ME! What kind of family is this? I am fragile. I can't take this."

He scuttles out of the living room and up the stairs, bellowing all the way. Sweetie is panting and shuddering at my feet. Her deafness is not protection enough. A door slams overhead.

Barbara stares at me, open-mouthed.

"You looked really scared," she says. "Were you scared?"

"Not scared of him," I say after a bit. "I'm scared of me. In that moment it took all my control not to put my hands around his turkey vulture neck. That's what scares me."

Alex comes to the living room to announce dinner. I ask if we can wait a few minutes.

"Sure, no problem."

Barbara and I sit close on the sofa.

"If Daddy were still alive and Doug had cancer, I know Doug wouldn't tell him until after."

"Thank you for that," I say. "Can I tell Dad? I think it will get him to listen."

Upstairs, Dad is hunched over like a gnome, inches from the blaring television.

"Get out! I don't want to see you! I don't want to talk about this! GO!"

Instead of obeying, I enter the room and sit quietly beside him. I turn off the set and tell him that Barbara has said that she and Douglas would have wanted to shield Bobby from bad news. It does catch his ear, but not enough to persuade him to come downstairs to eat with us.

Barbara and I start dinner without him. After ten minutes, Alex can't stand it any longer and tiptoes upstairs to talk to Dad. They come down together, and Dad takes his place at the head of the table. We make light conversation while he eats, and, back in raconteur mode, he recites an old ditty that used to make Bobby laugh.

> There was a young man named Bruno
> who'd make love to anything you know.
> A young girl was fine,
> a llama divine,
> but a vicuna was numero uno.

Barbara is able to respond with simulated amusement, but I am wiped out.

The next evening, a Friday, marks the end of Mom's fifth day of hospitalization. The intrusive therapies offer harassment, not healing. At least there won't be therapy over the weekend. I phone Dad from the medical center to tell him that I can't visit.

"I have to get home to go to our friend Jeff Simon's sixtieth birthday party."

"That's okay," says Dad. "Tonight I'm taking Louise to the Ritz for dinner."

My reaction to his announcement is delayed. I feel nothing until a couple of hours later, when Jeff comes up to me at his party.

"Oh, Pat, I'm so sorry to hear about your mother. How is your poor father doing?"

I hear my disembodied voice say, "Oh, he's fine. He's taking his old girlfriend to dinner at the Ritz."

End Game

Each day prolongs Mom's ordeal. Peter and I have been unable to disabuse Dad of his unrealistic and grandiose home-care schemes. Not until Friday, September 11, do we get an appointment with Dr. Anderson, the geriatric psychiatrist. He is our last hope for getting Dad to consider Mom's needs.

Instead, it offers one more opportunity for Dad to publicly proclaim all the reasons he does not like Peter.

"I know I have a poor disposition and an emotional immaturity," Dad begins. "My impatience and anger take over. That's my nature, and it causes me much trouble. I can admit my faults. Now, if I discuss things with you, Peter, flags go up, and you immediately become the devil's advocate."

"Dad, your anger turns me off. You have agendas. I feel prejudged. I want to flee."

"You exacerbate it. You take the other person's side automatically. I can't be open with you. I want to be able to talk about things on my mind. I wish you would see a therapist the way Pat and your mother do to learn better ways to deal with me."

"Dad, that's outra—" I try to break in.

"I don't like it," Dad drowns me out, "when Peter calls me Hank and Henny Boy in that cutesy, phony voice."

Just as I am silently vowing never to let Dad publicly denounce Peter ever again, Peter turns to me and asks,

"Pat, what's it like for you to always be the one to run interference? You've spent your life trying to make everyone happy."

Without hesitation I am lucid and spontaneous. "I just realized that I have reached the age of retirement. I don't have to do this anymore!"

We then get to the matter at hand: how to bring Mom home to die as humanely as possible. Dad is finally forced to accept the inevitable.

"I've needed help controlling my disposition, but I can provide what Carol needs now. I want what's best for her. If you pull the plug, I'd rather have her home."

"And in her own bed in your bedroom?" I ask.

"Whatever you say."

The session ends with Dad agreeing to meet weekly with Dr. Anderson on his own. As we are filing out of the office and beginning our descent down the long, narrow staircase, Dad turns to Peter and says, "Did I tell you the one about—"

Peter says, "Dad, I don't want to hear a joke. This is not the time."

The next morning, Saturday, twelve days after the stroke, an ambulance brings Mom home. I like to think she knows where she is. Bright sunshine beams through the bedroom curtains. Alex and Josie have picked and arranged bouquets of her roses. Sweetie jumps on her bed and curls up beside her, not to be dislodged. Kate flies in from Los Angeles. Peter and Beverly, Ron, Alex, Josie, and the hospice nurse are there. I feel sad and awed, but find comfort in our being together. Only Dad is unable to connect. He paces the hall, complaining audibly about being relegated to sleeping in my bedroom.

Mom takes her last breath at 11:40 AM the next day, Sunday, September 15.

We are at her bedside, but Dad shuffles restlessly on the outskirts.

"These are the last people I want to be here," he mutters.

A short time later Sweetie emits a howl unlike any we have ever heard. She jumps off Mom's bed, never to lie there again.

While others spring into action, Beverly and I stay with Mom. Ron and Peter take Dad to visit Marjorie, the last of the sisters. I slip Mom's engagement and wedding rings from her finger. Then I wait for the funeral home agents to come and take her away. I don't want her to be alone. It is terrible to give her to strangers and to watch as they carry the wafer-light bundle on a stretcher down three flights of stairs, out the front door of the house she adored, and into the back of a van.

There is not a moment to mourn. We have an obituary to write, which Peter does, and a memorial service to convene, which I do. We hold a high tea at home for family and friends. It is a sunny afternoon, the kind Mom lived for. She would have approved of the luscious bouquets of garden flowers and the platters of tea sandwiches arranged like mosaics.

"How do you do this with dry eyes?" asks tear-streaked Kate, who speaks after me. She tells how Mom had always been her best friend despite their age difference.

She points out how ironic it is that we should be remembering someone who hated funerals, hated speeches, and always wanted to be somewhere else. "So, in memory of my grandmother, would everyone please imagine where they would rather be."

Follow the Leader

A few days after the memorial service, Dad asks me to be his social secretary.

"I want to start having dinner parties. We can invite the Greens and the Fields and Lou. You can be the hostess."

"Dad, I don't think I'm ready just yet."

"Oh, you mean you're still mourning?"

"Well, yes, I guess you could call it that."

Dad's rush of activity prohibits mourning. He keeps all of us spinning. First thing, he has Josie throw out all of Mom's basket-making and collage materials.

"What a bunch of junk!"

I am stunned. In the '70s and '80s Dad took pride in the prominence Mom won from the art world. He enjoyed her gallery openings and museum galas. While he valued her finished products, he took no interest in her process. It is too late now for me to object.

With Peter's prostatectomy approaching, Dad makes audiotapes detailing his own prostate history. He underwent a procedure in his seventies that left him impotent and cannot understand why this story fails to comfort Peter.

"I've tried very hard with your brother. He avoids me like the plague."

I no longer try to explain. In fact there is too much I cannot explain. Josie reports mysterious nocturnal activity. Sometimes when she comes to the kitchen to start breakfast, the stove's gas knobs have been left on. Often, during the night, the electric garage door opens and closes. One morning it was found open.

Josie's bedroom is off a back hall that connects to the garage. She hears someone turning her doorknob in the night. Could it be Miss Carol's restless ghost? Josie is too frightened to tell Dad, but she agrees to use the alarm system regularly after Dad has gone to bed for the night.

Very gradually, over the next few weeks, Dad's visits to Dr. Anderson bring some relief. Dr. Anderson has prescribed Depakote, an antiseizure medication for epileptics. It is the first drug that Dad can tolerate without side effects, and it does help to delay or subdue his rages. Now Dad likes Dr. Anderson so much that he makes him audiotapes to listen to between sessions. I don't know how Dr. Anderson responds, but taping himself fills Dad's lonely hours. He makes additional tapes for Peter.

Peter comes through his prostate surgery bravely and convalesces under Beverly's watchful care. Soon he visits Dad with increasing frequency and does countless errands that require a car. Things are going so well that Ron and I take our kids to Costa Rica for Thanksgiving vacation.

We come home to a scene of utter calamity. While we were gone, Sweetie became violently ill. Peter took her to the vet each day and brought her home to Henry each night as he insisted. On the last night of her life Dad stayed up with her until dawn as she retched and shat all over the upstairs TV room.

The very next day, only hours after Sweetie's death, Dad's next-door neighbor, a trustee of the San Francisco SPCA, brought him Tiger, a small Yorkshire terrier mix. By the time I get back from Costa Rica, Sweetie is gone and already replaced, and Dad is suddenly no longer on speaking terms with Peter. Peter faxes me a copy of a letter he's written to Dad.

February 13, 2002

Dear Pop:

I am sorry that you are so upset with me that you neither want to see nor talk with me. As I said, I am happy to talk with you anytime. I want you to know that my decision not to listen to more tape recordings does NOT mean that I am not interested in your thoughts, only in the method of delivery. At my age, and yours, I feel we should still be able to have a reasonable conversation and not depend on one way declarations, whether by tape, letter or fax.

I regret that I somehow enraged you on Tuesday afternoon. I want you to know that I only came over to help. Tiger is a sweet dog and I certainly wanted to make sure she got the attention she needed.

I know it has been a tough year for you. It hasn't been the best for me, either, but that is not really the issue as we look ahead. With the losses of Carol and Sweetie, I would hope you would value the family ties that still remain. I know how much I appreciate my relationship and friendship with Adam and Daniel and I would like, even at this

221

late stage, to have a better relationship with you. Perhaps I have not been the son you wanted, but I'm the only son you have. I hope you can find it in your heart to try and re-establish a better relationship with me. If yes, great. If not, I think that would be very sad for both of us.

In any case here is a cute Jewish joke (that you have probably already heard).

Abraham the Yarn Merchant

Abraham, an old Jewish immigrant, sells imported yarn. He lives in New Jersey next door to the biggest anti-Semite in town. One day the anti-Semite calls up Abraham and says, "Hey, Jew! I want to buy a piece of orange yarn. The length must be from the tip of your nose to the tip of your penis, and I want it delivered tomorrow."

"Okay," says Abe.

The next morning the anti-Semite is awoken at six AM by the sound of trucks. He runs outside to see the trucks dumping truckload after truckload of orange yarn in his front yard. Soon the yard is a sea of orange yarn five feet deep. Abe then presents a bill for $12,000 to the anti-Semite.

The guy starts yelling and screaming at Abe.

"Jew, what are you doing to me? I asked you for a piece of yarn from the end of your nose to the tip of your penis. Look at this place. What do you have to say for yourself?"

Abe replies, "The tip of my penis is in Poland."

Ring Around the Rosie

Just as I am steeling myself for Dad's worst, his better angel appears. He's chafing to do something in Mom's memory: "How about establishing a chair in textiles at Mills College. Would you look into this for me?"

Peter is willing, and I am thrilled to have a constructive project to bind us. We quickly learn that it takes millions, not thousands, to set up an academic chair, and Mills College has no interest in textiles. We offer Dad a number of ways to structure his gift. Instead of putting it all in one project, we suggest several.

"No, not those," he interrupts. "I want ACLU!"

"That was at the top of my list," I say, "but I didn't think you'd go for it."

On the day that Dad delivers his gift in Mom's memory to the ACLU, Peter and I take him out for lunch. He explains his philosophy of money:

"If you make it yourself, you can do anything you want with it. But money you inherit is like a tree. You can enjoy the fruit but never kill the tree. You inherited it, and someone else should inherit it from you. You can pick the fruit while you are alive, but don't spend the principal. What you inherit is for the next generations."

Dad worries that he is losing weight. To regain it, he stops smoking! Cold turkey. The man with no self-control quits a lifetime habit. He sucks Nicorette lozenges, applies

Nicoderm patches, and never again takes another puff.

"Much harder than giving up alcohol," he says.

His strength of will put to good use impresses me.

Dad is lonely. He spends days sifting through boxes of old letters and memorabilia. He is hurt that Mom threw out all the letters he wrote to her during the War. He saved all of hers.

"She hated me. At the end she really hated me."

He is seeing clearly. I cannot summon words of comfort.

Some days we endure setbacks.

Blowout #1: Inadvertently, Peter provokes a tantrum after the microwave oven shorted out. To surprise Dad, he installs a brand new one, which has a flat control panel instead of buttons.

"How could you give a blind man a machine without buttons?" he roars. "Why didn't you tell me? Where is the old one? How could you deceive me? You have taken away my independence."

It takes Dad two days to get over this.

"I want a tax deduction for the old one!"

Blowout #2: Five days before Christmas 2003, Dad complains to me over dinner that he wants to clear out the high closet shelves where Mom stored all the unsold baskets she'd made. None of us knows how many are up there. They are so far out of reach that we've been lazy about getting a ladder to go up and see.

"Let's get them down before Christmas so the family can make selections before we give them to the craft museum," says Dad.

"Great idea!" I agree. This will be the first time since Mom's death that all of their grandchildren will be together.

Early the next morning Josie phones in a hushed, urgent voice.

"Pat, Pat! The baskets are all gone. The museum ladies have just come and taken them away."

"What? That's impossible. Last night Dad agreed to wait until after Christmas before calling the craft museum. I had no idea they were coming so soon."

"I know. They didn't want to. One asked, 'Are you sure this is all right with the family?' And Sir Henry said, 'Yes, yes. Take them. Take them.'"

I immediately phone Peter, whom Josie has already alerted. He drives straight to the museum and gets them all back. There are so many they hardly fit in his car.

I phone Dad enraged.

"How could you—"

"Listen to me, goddamnit. I've been waiting months. She's been dead fifteen months, and I'm waiting here all this time. Stop utzing me."

"Dad, I didn't know this was such a burden."

"Like hell! You could've looked. I've never seen so much crap in my life. What a mess! It filled boxes and boxes."

"Dad, this is art. It's Mom's creative life."

"Shut up. I don't want to hear—"

"Dad, it's her legacy."

And then I snap. The person I want to be, his self-appointed savior, is incinerated. Everything I've struggled to become is stripped away—my kindness, my patience, my self-control. Once again I am falling into the dark hole of his despair, sinking fast. There are no handholds of reason to grab onto, no Mom or Peter to inhibit my fall. At this speed nothing can stop me. I am hurtling down, going all the way to the hell he inhabits. And when I hit rock bottom, I steal another favorite practice from his playbook: shaking with rage, I hang up on him. How can I be doing this? How can he?

Christmas dinner takes place a few days later at Peter and Beverly's. Daniel is back from the Peace Corps in Guatemala; our son, Peter, from Argentina; Adam and Eileen from Japan. Dad and I make no mention of our confrontation. Everyone brings delicious food. Dad is so full that he collapses on the living room couch and takes a long nap after dinner.

While he sleeps, the rest of us tiptoe to the garage to bring the bulky boxes of Mom's baskets upstairs to Peter's study. Dad is oblivious to our activity as we dive like grave robbers into the cartons of salvaged treasure. There are baskets stuffed inside of baskets. Nothing is wrapped with care. There must be fifty pieces, all jumbled randomly.

Quietly we pick up the whimsical baskets to examine them. Cousins Paul and Kathy hold some eggshell-thin paper bowls up to the light. They glow.

"Pat, these are beautiful. You must keep them," says Paul.

"No, no. I want you to take what you want."

"Really, you must do something with these."

Much later, after all have made their selections, I pack up what's left and take them home to Berkeley. I vow to write a tribute to Mom that will be a professionally photographed catalog of her work. I have Dad to thank for provoking me into action. The book, *Carol Sinton, Fiber Artist*, becomes an act of sweet revenge.

Blowout #3: Between Dad's tirades are periods of calm. I am comforted to know that he has some social life outside the family. He still sees Lou and Louise, and almost every week Josie invites company to dinner.

Just when I am letting down my guard, the peace is shattered. Josie phones:

"Pat, last night Sir Henry and Louise had a big fight. She walked out in the middle of dinner. I think they have broken up. Your father is very upset."

I drive to the house, and Dad is eager to tell the story.

"Over dinner I was telling Louise how much I appreciate all that Josie does for me. I couldn't be living in this big house without her. To thank her I'm planning to leave her $10,000 in my will.

"'Well, Henry, that's very nice,' says Louise. 'I've been wondering, what are you leaving me?'

"So I say to her, 'Louise, I prefer to give you gifts while I am still alive.' Then she gets all put out because she thinks she's entitled to the same respect as Josie and maybe more, given the forty-plus years we've known each other. I put my foot in it when I tell her it's an embarrassing relationship. She throws down her napkin and says, 'You make me feel like a whore.' Then, just as she's about to storm out of the house, I say, 'Louise, if you're a whore, you're the most overpaid, underfucked whore there ever was.'"

"Dad, you didn't!"

"Yes. And now she won't answer her phone, so I have to leave messages. Maybe you could take down a letter for me? I'm returning all the stereo equipment and CDs she gave me."

Dear Louise,

I am returning these gifts because they remind me too strongly of you who I am trying so hard to forget.

This is not the outcome Peter and I expected. We assumed Dad would provide for Louise in his will. We never imagined this.

"You and Peter both behaved very well regarding Louise. You never criticized me."

"Dad, it wasn't our business. You're an adult. It's your life."

"Well, I'm telling you: I appreciate it."

Dad's life after Louise is more lonely and contemplative. He turns to me to be his mother confessor:

"Your mother is the first girl I ever liked. I needed her and clung to her. She had a wonderful personality and sense of humor and a beautiful figure. I was crazy about her. I had no sexual experience before her. I lucked out; we both lucked out in a sense.

"We were immature. I had no pinfeathers yet. Stanley was my idol, and chasing girls was a sport for him.

228

The first time I was unfaithful was in 1942. Carol was at Tahoe with you. I took a secretary from the navy supply depot out to dinner, and she practically raped me. I felt so guilty. I couldn't wait to get to Tahoe to confess all to Carol, my best friend. But instead of understanding, she went hysterical.

"'You horse's ass! Next time keep it to yourself.'

"It made me mad. People don't find solutions outside of marriage, only inside marriage. Your mother could cut me out. Still, I miss her very much, but not the last years. She started pushing me away as my eyes deteriorated. She didn't want me to be dependent. She used my infidelity as a justification.

"Oh, Patchy, remember that time you came to me instead of your mother when you'd gotten seam squirrels? That made us friends. You came to the right person. You got a cure, not a lecture.

"You said, 'Dad, I have an itch. What're these?'

"And I sang you that song:

> Put on the old blue ointment
> to the crabs disappointment.
> Take a hot bath every other day.
> Christ, how it itches,
> but it kills the sonsofbitches
> in the good, old-fashioned way!

"And I gave you something better: Larkspur Lotion."

He Loves Me, He Loves Me Not

May 25, 2004

For sixty-four years I have known this moment would come, yet I am unprepared. I am caught neglecting Dad. I am in Maui with Ron. On our second morning there, urgent predawn calls from Peter and Josie inform us that Dad's nights have become worse than his days. He is getting up constantly to go to the bathroom and woke Josie six times last night and numerous times the night before. Ron suspects that a polyp in his colon, which Dad chose not to treat, might be causing an obstruction.

We fly home and are surprised to be met by Kate at the airport. She had arrived earlier in the day and had spent an hour and a half with Dad while he entertained her with stories. She tells us of two tender moments. He said, "Our family has been very lucky, all of us. I've dodged a lot of bullets." And then he told her, "Kate, I am going to miss you."

I am so relieved that he is still alive and cogent.

We spend the next day, Tuesday, trying to get Dad diagnosed and to alert hospice. His kind internist pays a house call that evening. Dad sits up on the side of the bed and tells a joke or two.

Ron comments that Medicare pays for hospice.

"Now you're talking," says Dad. "Tell them to put me on life support 'til after the election. I can't die under a Bush."

When I leave to go home, Dad says, "I am a generous person, and I am dog tired."

A bad night follows. Josie and I try with mounting desperation to get through to the Jewish Family Service, but the Shavuot holiday closes down the place. Not even an answering machine functions. I cannot leave a message. We have to resort to other agencies and start from scratch to set up hospice.

Thursday dawns ominously. Dad and Josie have been up all night. Dad is in diapers, hemorrhaging. He doesn't want to soil his bed and struggles against us to get to the bathroom. I try to keep him in bed, but he is combative.

"Pat, you're a goddamned nuisance," he yells. "Get out! Get out! You're stubborn. I shouldn't have to suffer like this."

I agree completely. Nothing is going as it should. Not until four in the afternoon do the hospice people arrive, one attendant and two administrators with reams of paperwork. While poor Dad is bleeding his life away on a commode in the middle of the bedroom, an administrator insists on conducting an intake interview. Adherence to paper protocol is hideous and dehumanizing, and I am no comfort to Dad. The heavy-duty medications don't come until evening.

Finally, around nine thirty, just after our son, Peter, has arrived, Dad starts to slow down. He wants to sit in his recliner chair and wear his shiny French leather shoes.

His speech is slurred, but he senses that Peter is present. He asks how long the drive from Santa Barbara took, and he mumbles something about a June insurance payment. He tries to tell a story, but it never leaves his lips.

I kiss Dad and tell him that we're going home to get some sleep.

His last words to me are, "Shut up."

Postscripts

At 10:34 in the morning on May 28 I am the one who watches Dad take his last breath. It is a lonely vigil at his bedside.

In the days that follow, when dialing the phone, my fingers automatically hit JOrdan 7-8490, Mom and Dad's number. I am jarred to hear Dad's robust voice on his answering machine. He's back! This is all a mistake.

Dad and Mom appear in my dreams. In one, I run into Mom at a summer social event. She has just had her hair done and is looking radiant, brightly dressed in resort wear, and very much alive. I am so happy to see her and tell all the latest family news.

"Adam has married Eileen, and they are expecting a child, due on Dad's birthday. Your grandson Peter has a wonderful girlfriend, Zoe. Oh, and Dad died last May 28."

"Really?" says Mom. "How did he take it?"

"Very badly."

"Typical," says Mom.

In the months before his death, Dad gave me burial instructions.

"I want my ashes to be mixed with Sweetie's in this box." He handed me an early American antique walnut box and a handful of favorite snapshots of him and Mom.

"Put these pictures in, too, and take the box to the Home of Peace. Place it beside my brothers in the Sinton family crypt."

"Okay," I promised breezily, never anticipating the obstacles that lay ahead.

Soon after Dad's death, I phone Judy at the Home of Peace Cemetery to tell her that my father, Henry Sinton, has died and that he wanted his ashes interred beside his brothers.

After a long pause Judy says, "There was no Henry Sinton."

"Yes, yes," I say. "He was my father."

"Well, I never met him."

"Henry was the youngest son of Stanley and Edna Sinton. He came to Home of Peace to visit them and his brothers, Stanley and Bobby. And Fred, who died when he was two."

"Oh, yes, I knew Robert. He was charming. He came in all the time with a gentleman named Ephraim Engelman. He made arrangements for Dr. Engelman's family to have the upper shelf on the right."

"My father, Henry, wants to be placed beside his brothers on the left shelf, I believe. How can this be arranged?"

Warmed by memories of Bobby, Judy relents, and Dad is allowed to ride to Eternity on Bobby's coattails.

But first I must find a proper container. Judy explains that wood rots and suggests plastic if I must do it myself.

My search for the perfect container takes me to kitchen supply stores (Pyrex canning jars—too exposed), to garden shops (handsome bronze planters—no lids), and to home design stores (a martini shaker—bad associations). Discouraged, I find myself absentmindedly wandering the aisles of Longs Drugs. As I pass the photography section, there it is: a photo box made of black plastic that resembles slate with a lid that is a picture frame! It is large enough to hold all of Dad's and Sweetie's ashes, and the snapshots fit perfectly into the frame.

Peter and I fill and seal the box and install it in the Sinton crypt at the Home of Peace on July 4, 2004.

One last rite is a postmortem with Dad's psychiatrist, Dr. Anderson. Peter and I are still trying to understand Dad. Most of what Dr. Anderson says is not new to us. Yes, Dad had a character disorder. He inhabited an emotion-based reality in which his impulses ran wild. He did express regrets to Dr. Anderson and was proud in the end to have controlled himself to the extent he had.

"You know who was the most important person in his life, don't you?" Dr. Anderson asks.

Peter and I freeze, afraid to guess.

"Who?" we ask in unison.

"Himself. He didn't have empathy."

Peter and I go to Baker Beach to digest this information. Baker Beach is the place where I find comfort. Dad and I often walked here together with our dogs.

"Where else can you find so much nature in the middle of a city!" he'd gloat.

Dad and I came to this beach for a heart-to-heart talk when I was fourteen. I was weeping over my nose. It was growing and taking over my face. I told him that I hated being ugly.

He said, "Patchy, you're perfectly nice looking. You're neither ugly nor beautiful. Your looks will never work against you."

I continued to sob. I wanted to be beautiful, but that moment of rare consolation with Dad might be why I still find solace in this place. Back then Dad did have empathy, selective empathy, for the favored few.

Peter and I amble from the Baker Beach parking lot toward the Golden Gate Bridge.

"I thought everyone had empathy," says Peter.

"Me, too," I agree, "just as I used to think everyone had a sense of humor. It's something we're born with, like fingers and toes. But some people do seem entirely humorless."

"Yeah, these things atrophy if they're not used."

"At least Dad had humor."

"But he neglected empathy."

I ask Peter, "I've always wondered why you stayed and endured Dad's abuse. Were you ever tempted to leave?"

"Yes, but I couldn't do that to you. I knew how terrible that would have been for you and Mom."

"You're right. Thank you for staying."

I lower my gaze to the smooth wet sand at our feet. The foamy edge of a receding wave reveals the silver glint of a coin. I pick up a dime. Peter finds a nickel and a penny. Another riffle of water comes and goes. A quarter, three dimes, and two nickels appear.

"Look!" we laugh. "Our inheritance!"

It is now eight years since Dad died. His noise reverberated in me long after he was gone. Ameliorating his torment gave meaning to my life. Writing these stories made me a more devoted daughter than I might otherwise have been. At times I stopped because it seemed unfair to scrutinize a person in old age. Is there a lesson here for the rest of us? How will we handle our dotage if we are lucky enough to get that far? Writing about Dad still shapes my days and keeps him alive for me in ways that I can control. This time around I get to have the last word—truly the worst form of purgatory I could imagine for Dad. He can't interrupt!

I come to the end of this project with a clarity I never had before. I've found value in having had a flawed father: Peter and I weren't burdened by trying to live up to a paragon. I've learned that favoritism hurts the favored as well as the unfavored. All my life I thought I was unjustly favored and therefore must pay. It felt unnatural not to jump when the phone rang and not to take on others' suffering as a daily practice.

I'm awed by the strength of family patterns. Perhaps that is why I still revisit the past, distilling it into digestible chapters, and wonder how Peter is able to walk away and sail unimpeded into a new life. He is free! And unapologetically happy!

I don't know if Mom and Dad would recognize Peter, who flourishes in their absence. Since his retirement from the *Chronicle*, he has become a docent at the Asian Art Museum, a collector of rare Japanese textiles, and a master beekeeper. He speaks expertly on all these subjects and spices them up with his own witty repartee.

Sometimes I tag along on Peter's Asian art docent tours and watch him attract an audience like a Pied Piper.

People respond to the enthusiasm in his voice. One time a growing crowd of listeners followed him into a narrow side gallery and got stuck. Peter eased them out of the cul-de-sac, saying, "This is like backing up a freight train." Would Dad be jealous or proud of Peter's ability to entertain a crowd?

Last year I dubbed Peter "King Bee" when he was elected president of the San Francisco Beekeepers Association. A beehive is a perfect matriarchy—a model of harmony and benign inequality. A healthy hive re-creates the world as it was meant to be: a place where the strong protect the weak and where each one performs the work expected.

I miss Mom and Dad most when times are good. I wish they could meet their great-grandchildren and know what a loving and engaged grandfather Peter is to Dylan (eight) and Alexander (five) and to Dan and Sabrina's newborn Juliana. Even Peter is surprised to find himself a child magnet. At playgrounds toddlers waddle over to climb into his lap and pet his beard. When he was younger, Dylan used to burst into tears of joy whenever Peter, his favorite, showed up unexpectedly.

In concluding this manuscript I can lay Dad to rest at last and follow Matias (five), Eleanor (three), and Zachary (two) toward a future I never thought I'd see. My new grandchildren unfold so naturally, brimming with curiosity and trust and individuality. I melt to see my own children becoming the informed, mature parents I'd always wanted. Each generation can choose to craft its own improvements. Peter and I were not fated to repeat the past. It is a gift to no longer live on high alert, treading cautiously and glancing over my shoulder, poised to dodge calamity. I am learning not to "walk backwards."

Mourner's Kaddish

Life is a Journey
Birth is a beginning,
And death a destination,
But life is a journey,
A going—a growing
From stage to stage.
From childhood to maturity
And youth to age,
From innocence to awareness
And ignorance to knowing,
From foolishness to discretion
And then perhaps to wisdom,
From weakness to strength
Or strength to weakness—
And, often, back again.
From health to sickness
And back, we pray, to health again.
From offense to forgiveness,
From loneliness to love,

From joy to gratitude,
From pain to compassion,
And grief to understanding—
From fear to faith,
From defeat to defeat to defeat—
Until, looking backward or ahead,
We see that victory lies
Not at some high place along the way
But in having made the journey,
Stage by stage—
A sacred pilgrimage,
Birth is a beginning
And death a destination,
But life is a journey,
A sacred pilgrimage
Made stage by stage—
From birth to death
To life everlasting.

Dad loved this Mourner's Kaddish.

Acknowledgments

Deep and verklempt gratitude to:

Peter, who stayed

Ron, who remains my indispensable in-house computer expert and love

My exceptional cousins, who lived these stories with me long before they found their way onto a page

Fellow workshop writers, under Jane Anne Staw's intuitive guidance, who goaded me on

Candid repeat readers, who didn't relent (Linda, Nancy, Jane Anne, Annegret, Barbara, Joan, Debbie, Kathy, Cristina, Maria, Bev, Jill, Madeleine, Lucy, Emily, and Zaza and the Wonderful Women)

Kate and Peter and their young families, who are charting a fresh course

Ilana Singer, whose Counter Conditioning Therapy taught me that I could disobey my deeply ingrained father-thought-voice

Designer Jan Camp, who turned these jagged chapters into something beautiful

Thank you.

About the Author

Pat Adler lives in Berkeley, California. Her stories have appeared in *The Berkeley Insider, BARk,* and in the Kensington Ladies' three books, *Ladies' Own Erotica* (1984), *Look Homeward Erotica* (1986), and *Sex, Death, and Other Distractions* (2002).

In addition to *My Father Who Is Not in Heaven,* Writers' Block has published *Fire in the Hills* (1992) and *Carol Sinton, Fiber Artist* (2006).

The book's title and subtitles are type-
set in Trade Gothic, with the author's
name in Garamond Narrow Bold.
Text is set in Adobe Caslon Pro, with
the protagonist's jokes in ITC Stone
Informal. Glyphs depicting bird and
moon are set in Cairo.

CPSIA information can be obtained at www.ICGtesting.com
Printed in the USA
BVOW020647190313

315750BV00005B/14/P

9 780963 416797